Distance Education, Instructional Design, and Ethics

Research, Theory, and Musings

ISAC ARTZI

Paperback ISBN: 978-0-578-00138-8

To my parents,
Frida and Haim Artzi

CONTENTS

Part I: Research on Learning

Part II: Instructional Design Theory

Part III: Technology and Learning

Part IV: Cyber-Ethics

Part 1

Research on Learning

On Historical Foundations and Philosophical Assumptions of Qualitative and Quantitative Methodology

Common understanding of qualitative and quantitative methodology is superficial when they do not take adequate account of the historical foundations and philosophical assumptions underlying both (Creswell, 2002). This essay compares and contrasts historical foundations and philosophical assumptions of qualitative and quantitative methodology, drawing upon the work of several different disciplines. A specific qualitative method is described in detail (a) how it works, (b) how conclusions are drawn from the data it generates, and (c) how the results are interpreted in the light of one of the disciplinary views described.

Introduction

Historical foundations and philosophical assumptions of qualitative and quantitative methodology are traced to current trends and future possibilities in theory development, application, testing, and evaluation. Creswell (2002) posits that the origins of quantitative methodology are in positivism, the belief that authentic knowledge is scientific knowledge. While there are many scientists who hold a similar position it is worth mentioning extensive work done by Ho Yu (2001) in which he makes a convincing argument to the contrary. Ho

Yu states that many debates between quantitative and qualitative theorists stem from the misconceptions about the positivist origin of quantitative methodology. Instead, Ho Yu describes a different relationship between logical analysis, and verification, for example, and quantitative methods. Ho You concludes that logical positivism, after playing indeed a central role in the developmental of quantitative methods has been overshadowed by the dynamism which typifies academic culture, social influences, and the broadening context of academic research. One should not necessarily view the disagreement between Creswell and Ho Yu as a conflict within the academic research community. Instead, this is a testimony to the richness and diversity in an increasingly sophisticated research environment. It is also an indication that current research methodologies originate in multiple disciplines. Educational researchers each bring their own pre-disposition to one branch or research or another and consequently present different perspective of their understanding of qualitative and quantitative methods.

Gall (2003) states that quantitative research assumes that the social environment is relatively constant across time and settings. Thus it assumes the existence of an independent reality which can be investigated. In contrast, qualitative research is interpretive and subjective to the meaning investigators attach to their analysis. Therefore a fundamental philosophical dichotomy is apparent in Gall's description: quantitative methods attempt to describe a given reality or uncover its governing principles; qualitative methods attempt to describe one's perception of reality and some aspects of its governing principles. Creswell (2002) supports these views by noting that quantitative research is usually an attempt to validate or invalidate a theory. The theory is assumed to provide the explanation to a phenomenon and it is assessed using data collected through observations and rational considerations. The elimination of bias is essential in quantitative research and to that effect standards of validity and reliability are set in place. Qualitative research is exploratory (Creswell 2002) and the data collected is open-ended, not guided by a specific theoretical assumption. The two approaches are not necessarily contradictory. It is possible for a research topic to be vague at first and thus warrant a more exploratory approach. Once more data is collected theory can be formulated and a quantitative approach maybe more adequate. These opinions point to an increasingly popular approach in research design, namely mixed methods. It is fair to assume that scientists, like all human beings have personal preferences. Thus, those who are more mathematically inclined (for example) may tend to promote quantitative methods. Others, may value more social approaches. The ongoing dialog among proponents of different methods may be indeed an indication that a convergent approach may be forming. Is there a need for such a convergence? The founders of modern scientific thought from the Renaissance to the 18th century (e.g. Galileo, Descartes, Spinoza, Kant, Newton, Hegel, Russell, Leibnitz, and others) could claim in their time that they knew everything there was to know in their respective fields. The amount of knowledge available today is beyond the capacity of any expert in any field. Consequently the process of scientific investigation must be based on cross disciplinary collaboration. This is manifested in the way research methods are evolving as well.

Salomon (1991) refers to qualitative studies as a systemic approach that assumes that elements of a study are interdependent and define each other in a transactional manner. Consequently he recommends studying patterns rather than single variables. Salomon contrasts this with the quantitative approach that assumes that complex (educational) phenomena can be broken into isolated variables, which can be studied separately. Salomon's observation is essential in the formulation of new design methodologies. The definition of variable is an research is likely to be influenced by the researcher's own bias. The clustering of several variables and the analysis of observable patterns is likely to reveal relationships otherwise lost in the separation between variables. It is also an opportunity for developing mathematical models for pattern modeling which could be more accurate as they take into account the simultaneous interaction among otherwise separate variables. MANCOVA is a definite component of such a design.

The problematic aspect of focusing on variables is further explained by Maxwell (1992), who found that there is a consensus among qualitative researchers regarding the impossibility of accounting for all individual activities, situations, or phenomena in a useful and credible manner. Maxwell believes that the process of defining variables in a study is influenced by external factors (the context of the study). Thus the variables do not accurately describe the internal relationships. Although statistical methods such as analysis of covariance (ANCOVA) are often employed to detect and quantify inter-dependencies they are only as good as the researchers' ability to define the appropriate variables. This however, can insert external bias. Constas (1992), while examining methods of qualitative and quantitative analysis, notes that most of the analytical procedures do not assume the form of specific rules. The guidelines are general and their applications are subject to the educational demands of a given study. The analysis of studies by Constas, Maxwell, and Salomon reveals a trend within the research community. On one hand, the mere use of sophisticated statistical methods does not guarantee a full understanding of all interaction between researcher-defined variables. On the other hand, qualitative methods are not sufficient to fully explain cause-and-effect relationships in an experiment. This realization demonstrates that the complementary nature of qualitative and quantitative methods has been implied since the earlier, foundational period of the respective research methodologies. The following examples draw upon work from several disciplines: Education, Health Sciences, Feminism, and Performance Assessment. These examples provide concrete context for discussing the ideas presented in this introduction. The post-examples discussion culminates with a focus and analysis of the method of collaborative research.

Discipline Example – Education

The educational field is ripe with examples of both quantitative and qualitative studies. Buchanan & Thomson (1973) employed a quantitative method to study the development of moral judgment in children. The researchers hypothesized that younger children use damage as the main factor in passing moral judgment, while older children focus on intent. The subjects were asked to listen to several stories and were given a scale to identify and rank instances of damage and intent and make moral judgment decisions. The hypothesis was confirmed using statistical analysis of the results. The authors stated that the quantitative judgment method employed by the subjects was chosen in order to minimize bias, a key concern in quantitative studies. Qualitative studies are often used to investigate in depth practices of particular individuals with the purpose of better understanding a particular characteristic or skill of teachers. An example of such a study is a doctoral dissertation by Brun (1992). In her study, Brun focuses on an elementary school principal who encourages teachers to assume leadership responsibilities. The data for the research was collected over a period of 16 weeks, with the researcher being a participant observer. The main sources of data for analysis were open-ended interviews, detailed field notes, and relevant school documents. The results describe teacher characteristics without an explicit ranking or quantification.

The first, quantitative study presented a dimensionally limited perspective of the problem. A set of variables were measured and a conclusion was drawn. The second, qualitative example clearly showed the potential for bias posed by the researcher's participation in the research. It also did not address a concern that participants in the experiment were more likely to acquire and display leadership skills simply due to the excitement in participation. Those who advocate this type of qualitative research would be hard pressed to explain how this method is sufficiently revealing in this case. Similarly, quantitative methods may not be sufficient to explain such complex issues as moral judgment in numeric terms as Buchanan & Thomson tried. Education as a discipline presents opportunities for investigating quantifiable variables such as test performance, as well as descriptive ones, such as depth of cognition. One should wonder whether the inclinations of some researchers towards quantification are trying to artificially impose quantitative methods onto subjects that are better described qualitatively?

Discipline Example - Health Sciences

Medicine is a field in which quantitative research methods are the overwhelmingly dominant approach for data collection and analysis. Banu (2001) describes a quantitative methodology for assessing chronic ulcers and scars in humans. The objective of the study was to correlate measurement of quantitative parameters (such as blood flow within scars) and results of conventional subjective clinical evaluations. The pilot study described revealed that it is possible to use non-invasive methods to measure biophysical parameters and thus assess severity and other characteristics of wounds. As noted by Maxwell (1992) this quantitative approach has indeed lent credibility to the findings. However, the choice of parameters was influenced by external factors, a source of potential bias due to investigators' experience and activities in the field. The extent to which the researchers were able to accurately identify representative parameters, directly affects the general nature of conclusions one can draw (e.g. extrapolated from ulcer to other types of internal wounds). A qualitative approach in this case would not have been adequate given the systemic complexity and structural nature of topic. One is therefore faced with the dilemma of measuring variables versus describing observation. Creswell (2002) points out the way of mixing the quantitative and qualitative methodologies in order to accommodate concerns expressed by advocates of one method over another.

This research example presents an opportunity to address several fundamental concepts in medical research and presentation of its results. For example one of the purposes of medical research is to compare treatment methods and recommend a best approach.

However, for some patients the best approach is the shortest; for others it is the least painful; for others yet it is the one covered by their insurance, while others simply trust their long-term physician to decide for them. The lack of understanding of these fundamental, social dimensions may present a distorted conclusion in a quantitative medical study like Banu (2001). Medical research is presented primarily to a medical audience, who is very biased towards technical efficiency and statistical proof of treatment efficacy. Consequently, this is a good illustration of the potential of a superficial consideration of social factors biasing the heavy reliance on statistical analysis. In a provocative way one could claim that life is the number one cause of death. It is definitely statistically provable. Following this provocative thought, should one then prevent death by treating its cause, life? This is obviously a ridiculous paradox, which demonstrates that a comprehensive treatment of quantitative and qualitative variables in an experiment would provide a better understanding of the problem and explain its solution in more sensible ways.

Discipline Example – Feminism

Interestingly, feminist studies are a topic on which researchers disagree regarding the applicability of quantitative methodology. Caprioli (2001) discusses the association between feminist scholarship on international relations (IR) and research methodology. She criticizes the current view that quantitative methods are not accepted within feminist research and consequentially it hinders, in her opinion, an objective treatment of topics like gender equality and social justice. Caprioli offers a path for reconciliation between errors stemming from misguided approach to feminist research and erroneous conclusions specifically in the field of feminist IR. Caprioli makes a powerful argument in observing the negative effects of the combination of gender bias, male-dominated politicians population, and a masculine, factual (who, what) approach to political science. This approach leads to political science being primarily about conflict, war, its management and avoidance. Caprioli argues that a quantitative methodology might reveal different aspects of IR, which would take into consideration and correlate feminist issues like inequality and focus on the human aspect of IR and not only on facts. The assumptions of the male dominated field of politics and IR are that the focus of research should be on the strategy of policy management. However, the feminist viewpoint is that compassion for human suffering and generally the impact of big politics on personal lives are examples of concrete variables measurable with quantitative methods. The current preference for interpretive methodology is more prone to personal bias. The domination of IR research by males perpetuates opinions based on perception rather than on facts. Caprioli brings as an example initiatives of micro-credit for women entrepreneurs in developing countries. In less developed societies, women are traditionally homebound and men are the ones with the responsibility and presumed skill to earn a living for the family. Quantitative research on women skills in financial planning and business management reveals that often women are as good as men or better in starting, managing, and growing businesses. Only quantitative methods can expose the true nature of the relationship between specific characteristics, talents, and feminist views and successful business management. Caprioli recommends that a continuous dialog should take place between IR scholars and feminist leaders. This dialogue would gradually bring about an enhancement of the explanatory capabilities of IR scholarship.

The discussion of feminist issues is an example of fundamental disagreements in research design in general. For example when one introduces gender as a variable in a research it is implied that the researcher believes it is interesting to see whether there are differences which can be attributed to gender. Why would a researcher believe this? Furthermore, should a researcher limit himself or herself to addressing gender differences only? What about eye color? What about religious affiliation? Height, weight or whether the last name starts with a vowel? The research presented by Caprioli is an example of (feminist) activism lobbying on behalf of statistical methods in research. There is an apparent disconnect between activism and statistics. However, a deeper reflection on this example needs to go back to the original purpose of research, namely to explain observed phenomena through various scientific methods. Researchers are part of the society we live in. In this society gender happens to be an issue in many areas, much more important than eye color for example. It is therefore to be expected that social issues would penetrate consciously and subconsciously the thinking process of research designers. The definition of variables in a study should avoid superficiality by making itself aware of the social context and qualitative metrics surrounding even the most carefully designed quantitative study. One could see a feminist agenda in quantitative research as correcting existing bias. On the other hand one could look at a feminist agenda as an example of other marginalized variables.

Discipline Example - Student Performance Assessment

The common practice for evaluating student performance in Internet-based classes is the assessment of regular submissions of written work. Some universities, like the University of Phoenix (UOPHX, 2006) require that students log on a minimum number of days each week and post meaningful comments on their peers' work. Daily written emails combined with larger weekly written assignments are for the most part the only tools online instructors are currently using to evaluate students' work. Some online schools, like Northcentral University (Northcentral, 2006) require that final thesis defense be conducted via video-conference precisely to eliminate the potential for impersonation. However, additional assistance and coaching which might take place at the student's location cannot be detected from the instructor site. Some instructors make an effort to interact with students often and give them the opportunity to comment or resubmit their work. The idea is that frequent interaction will acquaint the instructor with a particular student's style of expression and thus increase the ability of detecting identity fraud.

There is an expectation that college education should culminate with a set of skills transferable to the real world and to the workplace. Already in 1991 Lehman and Granger reported that Empire State College specifically addressed the evaluation issues raised by an individualized educational program for adults. Empire State's program provided for an individually designed degree plan and learning contracts. In a fundamental sense, an individualized educational program required an individualized assessment strategy (Hodgkinson, 1975). Lehman and Granger observed that as recent as 1991 individualized assessment seemed prohibitively difficult and expensive for most colleges.

Behaviorist learning approaches advocate the principle of practice at performance criteria. These criteria are the result of reconciling two sets of requirements. The first is that presented by a student's current or potential future career. The second is the expression of a student's personal goals. In the absence of concrete personal objectives or outside dictated ones it would be impossible to assess whether a student has successfully completed a task or passed a course.

Rossman wrote in 2002 in support of individualized assessment that in time our mass-produced standard subject-matter tests would be replaced with individualized testing that adequately takes account of unique learning style, talents, opportunities, needs, handicaps, limitations diagnosis. The modularity of Internet-based instruction can lead to a true assessment of student performance in comparison with stated objectives and success criteria. As long as these criteria are clearly stated and an agreed upon interpretation of evaluation results is established the road is open for individualized assessment.

The above examples highlight the interest in developing personalized learning and assessment methods in education. From the perspective of understanding the philosophical assumptions of quantitative and qualitative research the interest in personalization requires a broader analysis. Personalization stems in part from the democratic belief in the universality of individual rights. The introduction of this belief in academic research is itself an expression of bias. A heterogeneous society like the American one might be more interested in individuality than say, Scotland. On the other hand, a developing homogeneous society may seek ways to increase diversity in education and assessment. From a socio-philosophical perspective, the research studies presented above are not addressing the root causes that made the researchers advocate personalization. The superficial belief that individual preferences lend themselves to individualized assessment and testing is not fully discussed and its need is far from proven. In a sense personalization is akin to a self-fulfilling prediction. It is obvious that if a student who does not like

Math is presented with an academic curriculum lacking Math classes, the student's overall performance will be greatly enhanced. The researchers do not make any effort in presenting the case for the interest of the society in the education of its members. From a research perspective this inserts such a large bias that it trumps the research findings. For example Rossman (2002) advocates the merits of individualized assessment but with disregard for the need for national standards of achievement. If the research, quantitative or qualitative, focuses only on the narrow benefits to the individual or a small community, it risks being simply irrelevant. This situation can be alleviated by the introduction of quantitatively measurable variables that not only describe effects on individuals but define success in a broader qualitatively expressed social context.

A Specific Qualitative Method – Collaborative Research in Education

It is interesting to take a look at collaborative research in education in the years immediately preceding the appearance of the Internet. Today the term collaboration has instant connotations to web-based activities, instant messaging, and video conferencing. However, before the Internet penetrated every aspect of research, the term collaboration had more theoretical meaning. Collaborative research is interesting because there are so many views about it and no specific set of universally applicable rules, as described in the following studies. There is no one method one could attribute exclusively to collaborative research. Consequently an explanation on how it works is contingent upon the specific mix of methods each collaborator is bringing. Collaborative research is best suited for cross-disciplinary studies where researchers with complementary areas of expertise form join teams, specifically for this discussion, academic researchers and teachers.

Hunsaker & Johnston (1992) define collaboration as a process where goals, procedures, and evaluation are defined jointly by the participants. Another attribute of collaboration according to Hunsaker & Johnston is the difficulty to implement it in practice. In the early 1990s there was a noticeable interest in conducting collaborative research in various areas of educational psychology, primarily involving academic researchers and school teachers. Koerner (1992) reports findings on collaboration between teachers and student teachers in elementary schools. Among other findings, Koerner notes that 75% of teachers welcome the opportunity to share classroom experiences with peers. While a small group of teachers felt territorial about their classroom environment, Koerner exposed a major purposed for conducting collaborative research – the need and ability to receive and provide ongoing feedback during the investigation and analysis phases. Koerner defines some attributes of collaborative research as an exchange of ideas and strategies that helps elucidate the gap in knowledge, how should the knowledge be acquired, and the development of motivational incentives for mutually beneficial collaboration.

Prawat (1991) illuminates another aspect of collaboration in educational research – teacher empowerment. In particular, Prawat addresses the epistemological approach to empowerment, which calls for teachers to examine their world from multiple perspectives. This examination would lead to the identification of new opportunities and bring about growth through collaboration. Educational researchers can empower teachers by complementing their field experience with theoretical frameworks for learning theory and instructional design. Prawat also describes work by McDonald (1986), in which he highlights the specific empowerment objectives of teachers: standardized communication language, collaboration with the academic research community, and placing individual achievement in a broader research context in the field.

In the pre-Internet era, Hunsaker & Johnson (1992) describe a case study involving an elementary school teacher who's teaching beliefs and practices have changed as a result of the collaborative research. The research was conducted over four years and had the purpose of documenting the changes that occurred as a result of collaboration. The research consisted of six phases: data collection, data analysis and interpretation, teachers' reflections, collaborative dialogues, and conclusions. The topics discussed focused on direct instructions, authoritarian management, and textbook-focused curriculum.

Another important aspect of collaborative research is that of conversation among participants. Hollingsworth (1992) addresses this issue in a description of a collaborative study she conducted, aimed at investigating about learning to teach. Hollingsworth points out that teachers value academic research in principle, but they see little relevance to their daily classroom activities. Hollingsworth's study concentrates on the feminist approach to collaborative conversation, but its implications are generalizable. For example, she describes the difficulty a male researcher would have in understanding the problems experienced by female teachers in a world dominated by male ideology. In a more general context, it is possible to assume that some teachers would have difficulty accepting theories developed by researchers that do not spend time in real classrooms situations, and therefore lack many of the experiences of the teacher. According to Hollingsworth this phenomenon contributes to an atmosphere of disbelief and hinders the development of collaborative conversation. In the described study, some solutions are presented. Two significant ones are identification of areas in which the teacher is also an expert, and creation of an atmosphere of shared learning

Denis & Lomas (2003) examine the academic roots of collaborative research and conclude that its purposes are: to broaden perspectives and offer a larger diversity of methodologies; improve interpretation of research results; increase reliance of research as a source for solution to problems; change the way researchers think; change the way research is applied; change the way society uses knowledge. Denis & Lomas identify the historical foundations of collaborative research as being participatory research, action research, program evaluation, and knowledge-utilization research. Collaboration helps frame problems from the often opposite perspective of researchers and practitioners. Through collaboration, these two groups offer a more balanced approach to problem space definition as well as to solutions and methods. Action research leads to knowledge accumulation (Denis & Lomas); participatory research recognizes the importance of collaboration.

In the earlier part of the 20th century, research was viewed as government sponsored activity. In 1970, The Rothschild Report (Denis & Lomas, 2003) established the distinction between basic and applied research, thus shifting some of the research responsibility away from the government to the scientific community. During the subsequent four decades the unprecedented growth in technology and scientific developments has gradually brought the scientific community to the realization that collaboration is a necessity dictated by the magnitude of knowledge accumulated, beyond the capability of a single individual researcher to process.

Conclusion

The implication of the examples cited above is that collaboration as a methodology has tangible research merits. Creswell's (2002) description of mixed methods research is a similarly supportive argument in favor of collaborative research. This could be translated for example into cross-disciplinary research teams, each using a different method for data collection and analysis. For example survey data could be cross-referenced with interview-spawned narratives to enable the examination of issues from two different mindsets: free flow thinking and choosing canned answers. This opens the possibility for the development of a next generation mixed method approach, in which statistical analysis of large data samples is used to validate or contradict qualitative, in-depth inquiries. A major implication of this trend is that the qualitative versus quantitative dilemma is diminishing in favor of a cross-disciplinary approach. Each problem is best solved if it is broken into several components. Each component is investigated by a researcher with specific, complementary, expertise in that area. Collectively (collaboratively) the group can produce a comprehensive analysis of the problem and suggest solutions. In education collaborative research presents unique opportunities in each study. For example a survey data on student performance can be collected and quantitative analysis can be performed by academic researchers. The results can then be validated by comparing them with information collected by teachers of these students, who know them personally. The mix of perspectives, personal by teachers, and abstract, detached by academic researchers is bound to yield results not envision or expected by one group alone. Every possible mix of approaches, beliefs, methods for collection, analysis and interpretation can be found in a given collaborative study. This aspect makes collaboration fascinating, unpredictable, and more likely to approach a problem from the multiple perspectives its understanding necessitates.

A Transactional Perspective for Adult Learning in the Context of Constructivist Learning Research Findings

A transactional perspective of adult learning posits that "a constructivist approach is necessary for learners to create meaning, and that collaboration is essential for creating and confirming knowledge" (Garrison & Archer, 2000, p. 4). This essay analyzes Garrison and Archer's transactional perspective for adult learning in the context of constructivist learning research findings. A case to use transactional perspectives of adult learning to research the impact of mobile learning environments is presented.

. Introduction

Garrison & Archer (2000) view adult learning as closely approximating the ideal learning situation they use in developing their transactional perspective. After examining the characteristics of adult learners, the authors concluded that three main groups of students fall into this category: working adults enrolled in academic degrees, graduate students (and to lesser extent undergraduate students), and knowledge workers enrolled in professional development programs. Their view supports the theory of constructivist learning, the ability of the brain to create new knowledge using pre-existing one (Huang,

2002). The framework proposed refers to the dual perspective – constructivist and collaborative – one can use to examine the learning process, or specifically in this case, the adult learning process. According to Garrison & Archer constructivism leads to creation of knowledge from inside whereas collaboration creates it from outside. The researchers thus distinguish between knowledge and meaning in a manner not entirely supported by constructivism. The process of learning consists of both the acquisition of knowledge and the ability to make logical inferences beyond the mere repletion of factual information. Garrison & Archer's model suggests that constructivism by itself only leads to the creation of meaning. However, they do not explain how meaning can be expressed without the context of knowledge.

Briefing on Constructivist Learning

Constructivist theory has developed gradually during the twentieth century (Huang, 2002) greatly as a result of research by Dewey (1916), Piaget (1973), Vygotsky (1978), and Bruner (1966). Dewey explored interactions between the learner and the surrounding environment and viewed learning through discovery as the preferred approach to achieve the goal of learning – improved reasoning abilities. Piaget concluded that educators play a central role in shaping the learners' experience. Vygotsky focused on the impact of social interactions on constructivist learning and proposed a social-constructivist model. Bruner added the technological dimension to constructivist learning emphasizing the importance of learning skills through technology. Judging from the information presented on most online learning institutions and their advertising campaigns of institutions like Capella University and the University of Phoenix Online, online learners are predominantly adult learners. Consequently, constructivist learning in online environments is particularly interesting in this analysis. Bruner's vision about the pivotal role of technology in learning makes him one of the de facto founders of technology-based distance education. Online learning environments are typified by asynchronous self-study and public sharing of ideas in discussion forums, but not so much by collaboration (although collaboration on projects is not uncommon). Garrison & Archer's transactional perspective seems to suggest that collaboration in an online learning environment is essential for knowledge to be created. If this assertion is correct, then online programs which focus exclusively on self-study, like The Open University of the UK and other open universities worldwide, should produce questionable results. Since many of these schools, especially in the UK and in the Netherlands are highly regarded, they seem to contradict Garrison & Archer's proposition.

Garrison & Archer correctly identify several groups of adult learners, like knowledge workers and graduate students. However, these populations have several key differentiating characteristics to the point which an equal treatment within a transactional perspective can be misleading. Knowledge workers within a company are more likely to be engaged in team projects and other collaborative activities. Even ad-hoc conversations on professional topics implicitly amount to a learning experience. In contrast, online students, even if asked to collaborate on projects, lack the team atmosphere and incentives as well the physical collaboration with peers. Thus one should question whether Garrison & Archer's transactional perspective adequately presents a balanced duality of requirements for learning processes: constructivism and collaboration.

Analysis of the Transactional Perspective in a Constructivist Context

Garrison & Archer ground their transactional perspective in part on Piaget's findings about the influence of educators and on his Cognitive Theory. However they view cognitive development as evolving beyond Piaget's stage of abstract thought, and continuing into adulthood. Brookfield (1995) clarifies this view by identifying four constructivist processes associated with adult learning: self-direction, goal setting, learning from experience, and learning to learn. Brookfield's finding that goal-setting is an adult learning characteristic parallels Garrison & Archer's second stage theme of responsibility. Self-direction and critical thinking are two processes identified by both Brookfield and Garrison & Archer. Without questioning the findings of Brookfield one could detect an internal contradiction in the attribution of a learning to learn process to adult learners. The term "adult" implies a certain level of maturity. Perhaps if one has not learned how to learn than he or she should not be labeled as an adult for learning purposes. One can extend this thought in a philosophical provocative way and suggest that from an academic and learning perspective not all adult learners are truly adults. An inverse analogy could be made to children, who upon experiencing traumatic events are forced by circumstances to mature quickly and thus display adult-like thinking and behavior.

Ozuah (2005) reviews the emergence of andragogy and traces its constructivist roots back to Alexander Kapp, who coined the term in 1833. Ouzah describes the seminal work conducted by Malcolm Knowles between 1959 and 1972 which articulated 6 basic assumptions about adult learning. Knowles' second assumption (Ozuah, 2005) is that adult learners are self directed and autonomous. Knowles does not explicitly support Garrison & Archer's perspective that collaboration is essential to knowledge creation, nor does Knowles corroborates that critical thinking is a key process observed in adult learners. He does however assume that learners are intrinsically motivated, rely on past experience to acquire new knowledge and make responsible choices about learning when they see a benefit. These assumptions are aligned with Garrison & Archer's themes of responsibility. Garrison & Archer explicitly cite Knowles as a source for their assertion regarding self-direction.

The treatment of adult learning in works by Ozuah, Knowles and Garrison & Archer, spanning four decades remarkably ignores the broader context of learning in adulthood. Whereas for young learners school is a central activity if not the main activity, adults must cope with fulltime jobs and parenthood, making learning a lower priority activity. It is also remarkable that the research works cited found that adults are more self-directed and more able to make responsible choices. Isn't this after all an obvious, universal characteristic of adulthood? It is puzzling that research findings emphasize on adult characteristics in a learning context as if they were not characteristics applicable to any adult activity. For example critical thinking manifests itself when adults make financial decisions, career path decisions, and other professional decisions at their respective work places. It is therefore to be expected that adults, being mature and experienced, will posses better ability to make choices and work towards completing their goals. It is therefore not entirely clear what contribution Garrison & Archer make towards advancing the knowledge about the learning process from a transactional perspective.

Korhonen (2004) is an advocate of an adult learning theory which matches Garrison & Archer's transactional perspective, but in the same time conflicts with parts of it. Simultaneous to presenting a strong case to support the notion of self-direction, Korhonen also presents results of a research which showed that 70% of adult learners do not necessarily seek meaningful learning experiences nor are they self-directed. Korhonen seeks to address the apparent contradiction with his own view by proposing that knowledge is indeed created in a collaborative process, but meaning and significance is attributed to individual perspective. In the search to find a constructivist corroboration of Garrison & Archer's transactional perspective, Korhonen's findings add a puzzling dimension. If, contrary to many other findings, adults are not necessarily self-directed then what does it say about the findings of any research on adult learning? One could interpret this as simply being a manifestation of the multitude of adult types and situations that exist in our society. If this is indeed the case then one should find studies that adult learning and thinking patterns cannot be generalized beyond specific affinity groups. This would relegate theories and models like Garrison & Archer's transactional perspective to secondary importance.

Fenwick (2000) explained learning from experience as a constructivist process, in which adult learners go through cycles of instructor-induced but self-directed critical thinking. The individual learning process is augmented by collaboration and exchanges with peers thus creating new knowledge. Belzer (2004) builds upon Fenwick's theoretical synthesis and adds the conditions necessary for the development of learner-centered pedagogies. Although Garrison & Archer never mention the term "learner-centered", their transactional perspective is focused on the learner. Thus it is possible to view the transactional perspective as an examination of another facet of learner-center pedagogy, or more adequately, andragogy. The difference in nuance is reflected by the researcher's perspective. One could view adult learning as driven by facilitators cognizant of adult learners' needs and thus enabling them to take charge; or one could view adult learners as driving the learning process from the onset, through informed choices and priority settings. Either perspective leads to a reality equally supported by Garrison & Archer's and other research findings presented above. Once engaged in an educational program, adult learners bring with them all past experiences, draw upon each other's wisdom and are proactive about collaborating and creating new individual and group knowledge. In this sense, Garrison & Archer's transactional perspective accurately describes a framework supported by other theorists and practical experiments. There is a pattern emerging from analyzing various studies which describe constructivist processes of adult learning. Every research focuses on a small group of learners and draws conclusions on the entire adult learner population. One would be hard pressed to believe, for example, that coal miners in their 50s going back to school to complete an Associate Degree have the same personal and professional objectives as hi-tech engineers going back to school to earn an MBA. Aside from the generic, obvious claim that both communities seek to advance and improve their professional prospects serious comparative research is necessary to improve our understanding of learning processes which would occur in these two hypothetical communities.

It is worth examining in greater depth the two end-processes of critical thinking and self-directed learning described by Garrison & Archer. Mezirow (1978), another prominent theorist, studied the experiences of women re-entering colleges. He observed that the women experienced a perspective transformation: they came back to college more driven, more focused on educational objectives. However, Mezirow (1978) did not mention collaboration as essential for creating knowledge. On the contrary, in a subsequent piece (Mezirow, 1981) he described a process of perspective transformation women underwent in the study. While Mezirow describes transformational learning as a process which occurs at the individual level, the engagement in dialogue with peers can be viewed as similar to Garrison & Archer's position that collaboration is essential for creating knowledge. When researchers like Garrison & Archer's propose a framework to help understand the process of learning it is understood and expected that their conclusions would contain a certain level of subjectivity. Given the diversity of the learner population, learner styles, learning environments, and research methods, it is sometimes possible to present multiple collections of research results which vary in their support (or lack thereof) of a given idea. The constraints of this discussion prevent a thorough verification of the acceptance of Garrison & Archer's position within the educational research community. However, other findings, by researchers frequently cited in current literature, lend credibility to Garrison & Archer's ideas, while others contradict it, as presented earlier. While education as a discipline is tolerant of dissenting opinions, other fields rely on unanimous agreement. For example, findings in Mathematics can be contradicted and discredited even by one counter-example, even if say, 99% of the research community shares the (ultimately wrong) opinion. The ideas behind constructivist learning and indeed those describing learning in general should be viewed as a temporary consensus opinion among a specific group of scientists rather than as a description of the actual processes which occur during learning. Such an approach allows for multiple frameworks to co-exist even if they are not in agreement, like behaviorism and cognitivism.

Whether Garrison & Archer's accurately describe adult learning processes is not as important as long as there is a credible body of research which supports their ideas even partially. The important fact is that their work along that of Knowles, Mezirow, Bruner, Piaget, Vygotsky, and other widely cited researchers, contributes to the understanding of adult learning. The ultimate test of the validity of these ideas is in the ability of instructional designers, learning facilitators, and educational administrators to use them to create learning environments conducive to the acquisition of desired learning competencies.

A Case Study of Transactional Perspective

The following example illustrates how a mobile learning environment helps make the case for a transactional perspective approach to adult learning. In this context, the mobile learning environment consists of laptop computers equipped with wireless broadband Internet access. The learners have access to a central, web-based learning center, which administers all learning activities and provides online collaborative tools. More specific technology tools available to learners are iTeamwork.com and Writely.com.

iTeamwork.com is an online project management tool. The site provides a system that keeps everyone notified on the status of a project while keeping the mechanics of the project management simple. Once a project is created, tasks are assigned to team members who are solely responsible for that task. An integral part to the system is email notification. Each team member as well as the project manager has great flexibility in controlling the flow of email. The team can receive a list of outstanding and upcoming tasks as often as daily. Project managers can receive notification of task completion as well as other task management duties.

Writely.com is an Internet-based word processor. It allows users to edit documents online and share them with whomever they choose, and then publish or add them to a blog. Writely.com users can easily co-create documents, store them online and access them from anywhere, anytime. Thus there is no need to email back and forth attachments and risk confusing document versions.

The combination of Internet-based collaborative writing, Internet-based project management, and wireless broadband on mobile devices creates an ideal mobile learning environment. Furthermore, it is a platform in which Garrison & Archer's transactional perspective and many constructivist learning principles can be tested. In order to make this case more realistic let us imagine a hypothetical project which would require several learners to utilize this system. A group of 5 graduate students are assigned to collaboratively write a 40-page research paper on "The Effects of Global Warming on Pelicans Migration". The students are geographically dispersed and are members of a virtual learning community. Each student is equipped with a laptop computer and has access to all the technologies described above. The students must decide who will gather data, how will it be shared with the rest of the team, how will the actual paper writing be divided among the team members, who will keep track of changes, etc. They are not sure how to distribute the load of work fairly and who will be in charge of managing and updating the most recent versions of the documents they create. The paper is due in four weeks and during that time they must continue work in other courses as well as earning a living in a part-time job.

Given the capabilities of iTeamwork.com and tasks identified by the team, the students implement a few operational steps and immediately start working on the project. The students create accounts on iTeamwork.com and Writely.com for the team and for the instructor. The instructor has administrator status so he or she can follow all students' activities. A new project is created in iTeamwork.com with entries for every required task identified by the team in an ad-hoc online meeting. Upon assignment of individual tasks, each student starts collecting and uploading results of observations of pelicans in their area as well as weather data. The team keeps an activity log created on Writely.com. Once a week, every team member adds an entry to the journal describing experiences, accomplishments, and summary of findings. The instructor also adds an entry at the end of each week that summarizes all course activity from a pedagogical perspective. The journal will be included as an appendix with the completed project. Once tasks have been defined, the team can start working. The team will use the Internet as the primary venue for research and collaboration; iTeamwork.com as the tool for managing tasks and activities; Writely.com for collaborative writing of the paper itself.

Theoretical and Pedagogical Implications of the Case Study

The creation of an intellectual product, like conducting a research study and creating a report, is akin to creating a product. The industrial concept of *product lifecycle management* or PLM, refers precisely to the type of activity described in this case study. The PLM perspective of collaborative learning is perhaps a missing dimension from Garrison & Archer's transactional perspective. The project described above is an instance of collaborative learning and social constructivist knowledge creation. Coupled with a managed approach borrowed from the manufacturing industry it can provide an ideal environment for testing different theories of learning in a mobile environment

A project or product management approach to online academic collaborative work can draw upon the vast body of know-how which has been accumulated over centuries of industrial planning, design, and manufacturing. In the process of managing their own work, virtual learning communities learn how to collaborate efficiently and how to assess fairness in the division of labor. In spite of the geographical dispersion of the online team and the physical distance from the instructor or supervisor, an Internet hosted project management solution offers a sense of commonality, security, and goal-oriented activity. Earlier studies cited showed some discrepancies regarding the self-directedness of adult learners. In this mobile environment the students have an opportunity to be very self-directed and manage a project or conversely be more reactive and complete tasks assigned to them by the project manager. Since all activities are performed under the scrutinizing eyes of peers and instructors in a collaborative environment one could define several important metrics helpful in understanding the learning processes at play. It would be interesting for example to observe whether otherwise slacking students are supported by the team and thus prevented from falling behind; whether it encourages high achievers to stay the course; and whether it helps team members synchronize their ideas, thinking process, and progress. Each student could be asked to maintain a personal journal in which he or she would document not only personal research findings but also personal thoughts about the learning experience. Since students would have continuous, mobile access to the Internet-based central project site, they could be encouraged to add entries to their journal as soon as a new thought comes to mind. Since these entries are automatically time-stamped researchers can use these data to compare personal progress and map it onto team progress. They can correlate personal experiences with the quality and quantity of contributions to the project site. An additional important metric is the amount and frequency of communication among team members. Researchers can thus investigate the impact of collaboration on the process of knowledge creation and compare it to the students' personal reflection journal and team contribution.

The sheer fact that all preliminary steps are visible to all relevant parties amounts to an de-facto formative evaluation of a course. The online journal is another major form of reflection, evaluation, and auditing tool. Since specific objectives, goals, deadlines, and responsibilities are defined at the start of the project, the end product contains all elements necessary for a summative evaluation. Both types of evaluation are embedded within the activities of individuals and the group and refer to all aspects of the course: content, instruction, collaboration, personal experience, suggestions for improvement.

Conclusion

Garrison & Archer presented a model for adult learning based on existing constructivist theory but coupled with an insistence on collaboration. Their research supports the notion that adults posses superior learning skills compared to younger ones. These skills manifest themselves in the form of increased drive, motivation and a sense of direction. While other research corroborated these findings, some studies implied that it is presumptuous to generalize about the adult learning population at large. The mere fact of a learner being an adult implies a richer body of life experiences, successes, failures, and experimentation. Thus the adult learner population is much more heterogeneous than the younger one. Adult learners, by virtue of them being adults are expected to be more responsible and aware of their own goals and responsibilities. In contrast, younger learners are typically enrolled in schools with more rigid sets of rules they must follow and are lead and supervised by both teachers and parents. Academic adult learning, especially Internet-based one, is a new phenomenon. In the absence of decades of studies in this specific area, researchers must build new learning theories and temporarily rely on existing research not necessarily conducted on similar subjects. Whether Garrison & Archer offer an accurate explanation to adult learning processes is still debatable. It is not debatable that the constructivist models of learning have sufficient support within the educational community to warrant a continuous refinement of its applicability to online-based adult learning environments.

Part 2

Instructional Design Theory

Instructional Design Theory Guides Decisions Made Relative to Reusable Learning Objects and Their Distribution

Instructional design concepts should lead the evolution of learning objects and particularly the use of distributed reusable learning objects (RLO). Lasseter and Rogers make the observation that "Deconstructing courses and reorganizing them as learning objects was technically straightforward...." (Lasseter & Rogers, p. 6). This statement is juxtaposed with the idea that "Instructional design theory, or instructional strategies and criteria for their application, must play a large role in the application of learning objects if they are to succeed in facilitating learning" (Wiley, D. A., p. 9). This essay analyzes some of the literature related to RLO and instructional design theory and synthesizes a statement and supporting arguments for instructional design theory guiding the decisions that are made relative to RLO and distribution of reusable-learning components.

Introduction

There are numerous definitions for reusable learning objects in the literature. The terms "reusable" and "object" are rooted in Computer Science and the paradigm of object oriented programming (Wiley, 2000). Object-based programming has revolutionized software engineering by prescribing that data and instructions should not be separated, but stored as standalone objects. In turn, these objects can be combined to form more complex modules. Thus the finished software product is a collection of objects, each with unique (but inheritable) properties, and functions (methods). The implementation of software objects is in the form of code (e.g. C++ or Java), which can be reused (via external linking or simply copy-paste). This evolution of software creation has been expanded to all technologies used on the Internet. Web browsers use the Document Object Model and the scripting languages are also object oriented (e.g. PHP, JavaScript, and XML). Some of the most popular and sophisticated web development environments such as Adobe Flash and its ActionScript language are object-oriented. It is natural to expect, therefore, that instructional designers and course developers should be influenced by object-orientation in their approach to creating educational content. Fortunately, an object-oriented approach to instructional design is not grounded in technology only. One of the fundamental strategies for learning, chunking, in effect advocates the braking of information and tasks into smaller units to foster memorization and commitment to long-term memory.

The discipline of Instructional Design is at the crossroads of instructional theory and technology. It serves as a conduit for mutual influences between theory and implementation. The concept of RLO is a perfect illustration of the fusion between theoretical principles and technological applications. The implementation of an RLO-based learning environment is a five-pronged approach, and assumes the existence of an RLO repository, an RLO classification system based on meta-data descriptions of content and purpose, an RLO search mechanism, a technology for combining RLO into larger educational modules and an instructional design methodology for building RLO-based learning modules.

Critical Analysis of RLO and Instructional Design Theory Literature

The literature on RLO consists of several types of work. Some discuss the merits of RLO; others describe technologies for creating and using RLO; yet others focus on standards that would make RLO use convenient and widespread. Few works, if any, describe a comprehensive, concrete, successful approach to design, implementation, and wide use of RLO. The works described and analyzed below were chosen to represent complementary aspects of the discourse surrounding RLO. The analysis makes the case that a comprehensive, cross-disciplinary approach to RLO design and implementation is essential for the success of the RLO vision.

Alonso et al (2005) describe an instructional model which implements learning objects and it is based on Merill's Component Display Theory (Merril, 1993) and Clark's research in cognitive psychology (Clark, 2003). Alonso et al propose an algorithm for learning based on the stages of analysis, design, development, implementation, execution, evaluation, and review. Learners who follow these stages interact with material that is dynamically selected by the learning facilitator. The model emphasizes the need for instructors to decide what and how to teach based on the classical content classification of facts, concepts, processes, procedures, and principles. The type of content and the teaching methodology is a decisive factor in the choice of appropriate learning objects. This model is very interesting from a design perspective and the detailed framework it provides. However, it is based on the assumption that a large RLO repository such as MERLOT (2006) exists. However, MERLOT is hardly a repository. It is more a loose collection of items contributed by RLO enthusiasts worldwide, without a unified structure, purpose, or standards. Alonso et al's work does little more than advocating the use of RLO in instruction. While they recognize the need to map types of knowledge (e.g. facts, concepts, skills, procedures) onto types of RLO they fail to explain how the mapping will be accomplished. Furthermore, they do not provide an instructional nor technological roadmap towards an implementation of their ideas. Nevertheless, their contribution is in the fact that they raise awareness and make the case for basing the design and use of RLO on existing theory like the classical Merill's Component Display.

Parrish (2004) proposes a model of Object Oriented Instructional Design (OOID) as a vector of innovation. He does not believe that it is realistic to expect that faculty will use RLO anytime soon. However, the OOID approach might lead to increased quality of digital instructional resources. He sees such resources as having repeated use. This is less than the reusability theoretical RLO call for but nevertheless a realistic step towards a future RLO-based model. Parrish's example is nothing more than taking a successful idea from Computer Science and explaining how in theory it could be successful in instructional design. While this work does not in itself contribute to the advancement of RLO design and development it does make an important observation. There are other disciplines that benefited from an object oriented approach and it is worth learning from them.

While many studies discuss the theoretical aspects of RLO, Bennett and McGee (2005) choose to focus on how RLO should be designed and used in view of the abundance of literature on how to create, store, and access them. To that effect they propose to think of RLO less in technical terms and more in conceptual ones. For example they suggest shifting from defining to designing objects. Bennett and McGee map the evolution of data storage and access technology and suggest a similar approach to RLO. Specifically they see the progression from document management systems, to data management systems, to content management and systems, and to cognitive attributes of stored content. The importance of Bennett and McGee's work is that they point to analogies to RLO in other disciplines and industries and show how a relatively young field, Instructional Design, can benefit from decades of accumulated experience in manufacturing industries. Bennett and McGee correctly point out the participatory and contributory aspect of Internet activities, both for education and entertainment. Consequently they allude to a social constructivist approach that should be taken into consideration when designing RLO. In their work Bennett and McGee have accomplished two important things. First, they established that RLO development is akin to manufacturing a modular, industrial product. Second, they emphasized the importance of design standards in order to fulfill the promise of reusability. Bennett and McGee go to a great length in explaining how RLO should be designed so that instructional designers could use repositories of ready-made objects to find the ones suitable for a particular course. However, the authors fail to address a trivial element that can hinder the use of RLO – the existence of a massive database. One could make the analogy between RLO and LEGO™ games. What use is there for a game with say, 10 categories of 20 pieces each, when there are thousands of structures that need to be built? The lack of discussion of the size of repositories prevents a true assessment of the merits of Bennett and McGee's work. One of the basic principles in engineering in general and software engineering in particular is scalability. If a model is only analyzed on a small scale what guarantee is there that it will work on a massive scale? It is quite possible that a group of 20 programmers and designers can be assembled to design RLO for one particular area. Is it feasible that the same group can design hundreds of objects within a reasonable time frame and budget? Furthermore, is it feasible that 100 additional such teams could be assembled to create a massive, cross-disciplinary RLO repository? The absence of a discussion on scalability relegates every study on the merits of RLO to the status of a hypothetical, idealistic idea.

An earlier attempt to design RLO based on instructional design theory is presented by Harden and Hart (2002). This example is important because the designers are from the medical field and the project described showcases the potential benefits between instructional designers, technology specialists, educational theorists, and medical professionals. Harden and Hart describe an approach implemented by the International Virtual Medical School (IVIMEDS). It is based on curriculum mapping, educational objectives, electronic study guides, peer-to-peer (constructivist) learning, and a bank of RLO. The authors view the advantages of RLO primarily in designing individualized learning programs, based on the background and goals of each student. Harden and Hart use Hodgins' (2002) LEGO™ metaphor to design curricula and instructional modules with reusable objects. The reusability is not only an efficiency factor, but it allows the creation of an interactive digital environment in which students can be easily referred back to modules they need to repeat for improved results. IVIMEDS also enables students to interact with the same learning object in different context thus providing great flexibility to course designers and broadening the students' experience. While not at the forefront of educational research, the report by Harden and Hart (2002) is very significant because it describes how educational needs and technological development are pressing educational researchers to develop new theories. It is very tempting for researchers like Hodgins (2002) who were discussing RLO in the earlier stage of their development to focus on their technological merits. The speed and fury with which the Internet has overtaken the educational and business communities has created an undesirable situation in which educational theorists are compelled to find theoretical grounds for using technologies they did not invent. Furthermore, Harden and Hart demonstrate that there is a great need for educational research to be conducted in the context of technology. The alternative is isolated efforts of technology enthusiasts with an interest in instructional design. Harden (2005) describes that in the four years since the initial article was written, IVIMEDS has grown to a network of 24 universities in 11 countries (IVIMEDS, 2006). The site contains over 1,500 peer reviewed RLO related to the cardiovascular system.

The work described by Harden highlights both the promise and challenge of RLO. The IVIMEDS project has indeed been successful in creating an impressive repository for a very narrow topic. The users of this repository are purportedly able to design many different educational modules, but not necessarily complete courses. The ability of the system to map RLO to individual students' needs and preferences is remarkable as well. It is also remarkable that 24 universities in 11 countries have participated in the project. Without negating the positive contribution of IVIMEDS to advancing the cause of RLO based learning and instructional design, one cannot overlook several critical problems with the project. Common sense dictates that the smaller the pieces (RLO) the more pieces one needs to create a meaningful structure (educational module). There is no indication as to whether 1,500 RLO are sufficient for the creation on 20 alternative modules or 200. As was the case with work cited earlier, IVIMEDS reminds of the feasibility problem of scalability. On one hand the project touts the numerous resources worldwide resources that went into its creation. On the other hand its use is limited to a very narrow topic, the cardiovascular system. It is easy to infer from this that were one to expand the concept to an entire medical curricula, pretty soon the only thing colleges of Medicine worldwide would have time to do, would be creating RLO. Naturally this is a ridiculous prospect, sufficient to cast a doubt on the viability of IVIMEDS as a concept. Finally, a random examination of the sites IVIMEDS lists as participants reveals many broken links and in some cases no reference to IVIMEDS. This could indicate that only a handful of the 24 sites were significant contributors and participants. It may also be a sign that some lost interest in the project or conversely have not taken yet the necessary steps in order to benefit from it. In summary, IVIMEDS appears to be nothing more than a limited effort by an enthusiastic few, although successful as a pilot program.

It is plausible that the absence in literature of a description of a fully functioning, large scale, RLO based learning environment stems from the fact that technology enthusiasts are moving far ahead of learning theorists and instructional designers. It is also plausible that a lot of theoretical work in the areas of developing new paradigms is required. In this context Wilhelm and Wilde (2005) describe the instructional design foundations for the development of an online course at Athabasca University, a prominent Canadian distance learning provider. After a multi-stage process which included an extensive search for learning objects, Wilhelm and Wilde found that the task was not efficient, time consuming, and would not result in the creation of a course based on their outlined instructional roadmap. Obstacles faced by technical and conceptual incompatibilities, copyrights, and unavailability of the exact content nuggets sought, led the authors to revert to an older paradigm – interactive textbook. Wilhelm and Wilde concluded that the failure to create a course using learning objects stemmed primarily from the lack of a sufficiently large pool of RLO. This conclusion is in line with findings cited earlier in this discussion. It appears that many proponents of RLO technology as the next generation instructional design assume that large repositories are widely available. Implicit in this assumption is the existence of many teams of developers that create thousands or perhaps tens of thousands of RLO for the general public. Such an endeavor is akin to developing open source software such as the Linux OS, the PHP language and the MySQL server. The traditional model of RLO as building blocks ready to be assembled was found not to be practical and too complex, long, and inefficient to be undertaken by an individual instructional designer. Implicit in this finding, and hence the pivotal importance of this article, is that theorists are limited to only dream-up sophisticated frameworks and pilot implementations. It is worth expanding this finding on a philosophical level and to briefly examine the analogy of RLO in Computer Science, namely to object oriented programming (OOP). Computer scientists and programmers have developed the concept of code objects to be used by other computer scientists and programmers. Whereas OOP as a concept and implementation is self-contained within the Computer Science community, RLO require intense collaboration of learning theorists, computer programmers, instructional designers, and content experts. Since it is rare that members of these communities have significant knowledge of each other's field it may be the case that the fundamental problem with RLO lies in identifying the right body of experts suitable for defining standards, developmental frameworks, usage frameworks, and storage. Until such a body emerges we are bound to continue to see local efforts of enthusiasts, sometimes driven by computer scientists with an interest in education or sometimes driven by education professionals with an interest in technology.

The absence of an authority that can steer the research and development efforts leads to sometimes adventurous initiatives. For example, Lasseter and Rogers (2004) deconstructed existing courses in WebCT Vista, converting each course into a collection of learning objects. This process took less time and was easier than they anticipated. The short term advantage of such an approach is that if the original courses were designed following a solid theoretical approach there is a good likelihood that the resulting LO would be of high quality as well. While they present a successful technical process, their findings do not shed enough light on the usefulness of the approach and the quality of instruction compared to the previous situation. It is also not clear who will update the RLO in the repository and who and how will new objects be created. Like with other research reports, Lasseter and Rogers are not clear about what is an RLO in their context. Thus this experiment only addresses the practical issue of how to kick start an RLO initiative, and this is no small feat, even if not significant enough for the field. The authors admit at the end of their report that the approach must be continuously marketed to faculty. This implies that its merits are not evident and the manipulation of RLO has not reached the desired user-friendliness level. These findings support the earlier claim that RLO design and development requires broad, long-term cross-disciplinary collaboration. A small team of educational technologists even if very driven and creative is limited in its ability to sell the idea to its larger parent institution. This is akin to hi-tech startups bringing to market innovative products no one has found the need for yet. Such limited efforts, even when successful, raise more questions than they answer. Who will drive the development? Who will pay for it? What courses are suitable for an RLO approach? Who will train current instructors in the use of RLO? What incentives would current instructors and instructional designers to spend time creating and learning how to use RLO? Evidently, since no large-scale, continuous implementation of RLO has been documented to date, may lead one to believe that many of these questions remain unanswered.

MacLaren (2004) cautions that any technology implementation should have learning as its primary objective. In particular he focuses on the tendency of educational software to emphasize presentation and delivery over learner engagement. Thus technological innovations do not always bring about improvement in learner performance although they improve the quality of the content. MacLaren is basing his recommendation on the conversational model described by Laurillard (2002). This model suggests that communication tools should be built around every educational module and avoid the superficiality and individuality (in Laurillard's opinion) common among computer aided learning (CAL) applications. MacLaren emphasizes a key element (often a flaw) in educational technology – most learners know how to use the technology but they do not know how to use it in an educational context. To that effect MacLaren presents an initiative at The Open University of the Netherlands, which defined an Educational Modeling Language (EML) to be used to describe learning objects. Using EML, instructional designers can add tags to objects to describe learning models (e.g. problem based learning), type of knowledge (e.g. concept, skill), expected competencies, and any other user defined tag that would emphasize the pedagogical objectives in the utilization of RLO.

An examination of MacLaren's propositions reveals a major obstacle RLO proponents must overcome: the insertion of a learning context within a technical concept. From a technological viewpoint, RLO are nuggets of code. From a content viewpoint RLO are nuggets of knowledge. The challenge is to create an object that is a nugget of both. MacLaren identifies and describes the problem in detail although he does not sufficiently explain how exactly to accomplish this. From the description of EML one can infer that a possible solution to creating RLO which are both nuggets of content and code is wrapping content with an EML-like descriptive (meta-data) layer. Alternatively, one could wrap the code with an EML-like content descriptive layer. The decision lies with the designers of the search mechanism for a given repository. If the search is content driven, then each RLO must advertise sufficient information so that an instructional designer can identify the most suitable one for a given situation. More specifically, it is fair to assume that the main users of RLO would be content rather than technology driven. Consequently, the RLO must appear to the outside world as content nugget, advertising sufficient information to facilitate an appropriate match with other objects. In concrete terms the RLO must contain descriptions about the type of knowledge (e.g. fact, concept, skill); it must contain descriptions about the level of content (e.g. beginner, advanced); it must also contain searchable keywords and tags that would allow one to use such parameters like title, author, discipline, or short description to name a few. Finally the inner layer, the one that makes an RLO a nugget of code in addition to being a nugget of content must include all the necessary hooks so that from a technological standpoint the RLO can be integrated within an existing educational module. Ultimately, the technical integration must be performed in a manner completely invisible to the non-technical user. MacLaren and The Open University of the Netherlands amount to a great first step in this direction but fall short of describing the comprehensive effort required by an actual implementation of their vision.

Metros (2005) also supports the position that RLO should be designed in a cross-disciplinary context, specifically one of knowledge management as opposed to content management as is the case with current learning management systems (LMS). In the course of designing RLO for an academic course, Metros teamed up instructional design and graphic design students. The outcome represented an emphasis on the graphical user interface (GUI) ergonomy in support of functionality, communication, and educational objectives. In an imaginary world, one could team up Metros with MacLaren and The Open University of the Netherlands to create a cross-disciplinary RLO design and development effort. Such a team would address the instructional design, graphic design, technology integration, and content integration imperative for the realization of the RLO vision.

Among the pieces surveyed, Hirumi (2005) stands out in his thorough analysis of influencing factors and guidelines required to achieve a high quality eLearning program. In the context of RLO, which he sees as an essential component of instructional design, he prescribes an approach that outlines standards for design and interoperability and for alignment of standards across the lifecycle of course development. Hirumi supports the view that there must be a uniform pedagogical approach that guides RLO design, their access and interoperability, all the way through designing an entire course. For example, Hirumi showcases motivation as a key concept in instructional design, but which is completely absent from the discourse surrounding RLO. Specifically he points out motivational factors like attention, relevance, confidence and satisfaction. The merits of Hirumi's contribution, like those of others described earlier are in pointing to yet another dimension of RLO design, theoretical foundations of instructional design. Essentially Hirumi describes what would make an RLO a good educational and learning module. However, he limits himself to calling for the definition of interoperability standards as a wrapping layer of the pedagogically sound content object. Hirumi leaves it up to the technical and instructional community at large to figure out how this could be done. If and when one does figure this out, Hirumi's guidelines could prove useful.

No literature review on RLO is complete without coverage of one of the few (if not the only) viable standard for RLO development, SCORM. The Sharable Content Object Reference Model (ADL, 2004) is a collection of standards and specifications for web-based learning. It is important to notice that SCORM started as a military project with the aim of making course design more efficient by promoting reusability through modularity. SCORM has piggybacked on the wide adoption of XML technologies to propose an XML-based approach to content tagging, wrapping and integration. Prominent content development tools like Macromedia (Adobe) have added to their products (e.g. Flash) the capability of creating SCORM-compliant modules. These are modules which contain a SCORM-XML wrapper that allows them to be easily integrated with SCORM compliant modules created with other tools. The concept of SCORM compliance has been extended to create SCORM compliant courses and learning management systems (e.g. Inquisiq EX and Results International). It is debatable whether SCORM is a good standard, whether Macromedia is a suitable tool for developing SCORM-compliant RLO, and what exactly is a SCORM compliant RLO. Contrary to popular belief SCORM does not define an RLO per se, only provides a framework primarily for reusability and integration. It is written primarily for vendors and toolmakers who build LMS so that all products are technically compatible. Given the increased adoption of SCORM by LMS vendors and the subsequent pressure on content developers to conform, there is an illusion that this is the long awaited savior of the RLO vision – the standard under which designers, developers, educators, and computer programmers will unite. If this was the case, than instructional design curricula would be abundant with courses on SCORM. The most thorough search of Capella University Instructional Design for Online Learning course description database fails to find a single reference to SCORM. Would SCORM be as popular among LMS technologists if they weren't starving for content developers to develop cross-compatible content? Would instructional designers in the heterogeneous world which is Educational Research have invented SCORM? The answers to these questions are anybody's guess. The fact remains that SCORM was a military initiative stemming from a centrally managed approach to resource utilization, cost and efficiency. As such it makes a powerful case in the context of RLO: there is an urgent need to establish an authoritarian consortium that would concentrate in its hands the entire cross disciplinary aspects of RLO research, design and development, implementation, and knowledge dissemination. There is at least one example of successful efforts which RLO enthusiasts could emulate: the Linux open source project.

Synthesis

The acronym RLO stands for Reusable Learning Object. Symbolically, the words "reusable" and "object" are borrowed from computer science (which borrowed them from manufacturing processes). The inner term, "learning" is the link between RLO and the world of education. Thus the term RLO contains within its description the essence of the desired development of its vision: an effort driven by the learning community wrapped in a technological framework. The literature examined earlier revealed efforts in different settings aimed at finding useful ways for implementing RLO. The analysis of this literature yields a set of four prerequisites for a successful RLO-driven initiative.

First, the only viable effort for defining, designing and building an RLO is one based on collaboration between the educational and the software development communities. Each one of these communities must contribute its requirements so that an RLO is simultaneously a content nugget and a code nugget, as discussed earlier. Within each one of the two communities a further division of labor is required. The educational research effort requires the collaboration and input of learning theorists and instructional designers. The software development community requires the collaboration of computer scientists and programmers. Since instructional designers should drive the educational aspect of RLO with input from theorists and since the educational community should drive the collaboration with software developers, it follows that the entire collaborative effort should be driven by instructional designers.

Second, a standard framework for the development, deployment, search, and discovery of learning objects needs to be defined. The existing SCORM standard is a good first step.

Additional steps require the development of a high level language that would enable non-programmers to create standard-compliant RLO. The final element of this framework should be based on SOAP (Simple Object Access Protocol). A SOAP-like protocol for RLO will allow the creation of web services to which RLO consumers would subscribe and thus RLO would be disseminated. The current SCORM development is driven by technical LMS developers, hence it is not perceived as an educational initiative within the educational community. In order to correct this situation, the initiative must shift towards instructional designers. They are uniquely positioned to act both as developers and educational theorists and thus promote the concept within the educational community. The promotion effort is essential in making RLO accessible to non-technical education professionals.

Third, in order for instructional designers and all education professionals to use RLO there must be an abundance of RLO to choose from. This implies the creation and maintenance of massive repositories, all containing standard-compliant objects and supported by web services for their delivery. The creation of massive databases implies the existence of large numbers of cross-disciplinary development teams. It is hard to say what is the desired threshold that would deem a repository useful. Using a naïve calculation of 10 objects per weekly course units, 10 week courses, and 20 courses per curricula there would be 2,000 objects needed for one curriculum. Obviously many institutions could collaborate towards the creation and exchange of 2,000 RLO in one area. In order to make RLO a household phenomenon across educational institutions one could envision that many curricula should be supported before the concept is adopted. It is anybody's guess how many different curricula are required to make an initial visible impact industry wide, but 10 seems like a good empirical guess. This would put the number of RLO at 20,000 just to call for initial attention to their viability.

Forth, an RLO consortium needs to be formed that would steer and manage all aspects of research, development, deployment and dissemination of RLO. The consortium must be driven by the instructional design perspective of RLO. Instructional design, although just one of the four disciplines recommended for RLO design and development, is the dominant one. Instructional designers are the bridge between the technological community and the educational community. Consequently they are best positioned to understand learning and educational requirements and translate them into technical functional specifications. Instructional designers are typically schooled in technical disciplines in addition to education. As such they are exposed to the mindset, issues, and trends surrounding RLO more than computer programmers or learning theorists, for example.

In summary it appears that the obstacles RLO proponents must overcome go beyond definitions or agreement on standards. The biggest challenge is feasibility coupled with a chicken and egg type problem. In order for RLO to be truly useful there must be many of them. There cannot be many of them unless people think they are useful and thus create many of them. The answer to overcoming this problem is utilizing the Internet and the massive number of potential contributors to RLO repositories currently working in educational institutions. The four prerequisites outlined above can be fulfilled by creating an Internet-based community process by which ad-hoc cross disciplinary teams can be formed. Such teams will use Internet-based tools to create standard-compliant RLO to be uploaded onto hundreds of servers forming a distributed network of RLO repositories. Instructional materials are today created by educators and teaching assistants at colleges and universities worldwide. An RLO consortium could steer the millions of educational content producers towards creating RLO based on the guidelines presented earlier. This is the only way by which viable, peer-reviewed, technically audited objects can be created. This effort must be driven at each location by instructional designers. Instructional Design is the only discipline that merges educational theory with technical applications. As such it is the only discipline currently qualified to be the center around which all other aspects of RLO gravitate.

The Impact of Various Implementations of Digital Learning Objects on Open and Distance Learning Practices

Koppi, Bogle and Bogle (2005) define learning objects as "discrete chunks of reusable learning materials or activities that can articulate with other learning objects to build a learning environment." Mackintosh, Mason and Oblinger (2005) state that "The extraordinary scale of education required today can only be provided through open and distance learning (ODL), hence learning objects and their promised scalability and reusability may fundamentally impact ODL theory and practice." This essay analyzes the impact of various implementations of digital learning objects on ODL practices. The construction and evaluation of a model for a self-adapting, personalized Internet-based learning environment using digital learning objects is presented.

Introduction

Learning objects may be a new concept in instructional design but there are many analogies in other disciplines. For example in software engineering the dominant programming languages are based on the concept of object oriented design. In real estate construction builders use such ready-made objects like doors, windows, and tiles to build or rebuild houses. The main reasons real and digital objects are used across disciplines and industries are efficiency, cost cutting, and scalability. Distance education is experiencing such a rapid growth that it is only natural that it should employ technologies that help it scale efficiently and cost effectively. The foundation of learning and instruction is Instructional Design. Open and Distance Learning (ODL) is a combination of distance education, online delivery, and self- study. ODL has its origins in the *open university* concept, like the Open University of the UK. It is currently transitioning into online (web based) distance learning. Digital learning objects are a fundamental concept in instructional design and as such they impact every aspect of instructional design for online learning and hence ODL practices.

Representative Implementations of LOs

The diversity literature on learning objects is a testimonial to the lack of consensus on what exactly constitutes a digital learning object. In this paper the focus is on LOs used in online learning and which offer a bit more "intelligence" than simple copying and pasting into an online lesson. A basic implementation of a digital LO is an XML document. For example, a quiz object might be implemented in the following way.

<quiz>

    <topic>Area of polygon</topic>
    <question>Given the following... etc.</question>

```
<answers>
        <choice1>36 cm²</choice1>
        <choice2>40 cm²</choice2>
        <choice3>52 cm²</choice3>
</answers>
</quiz>
```

Another commonly used model for learning objects is the Java applet. This type of object utilizes the rich functionality of the Java programming language and its ability to interact with other network and browser objects. The example below shows how such integration might be implemented over the Internet:

```
<object classid="clsid:8AC840-044E-111-B39-
005F499D93"
        width="200" height="200">
         <param name="code"
        value="http://www.capella.edu/objects/gravity.class"
         >
</object>
```

The applet *gravity.class* is presumably in an online repository and is included in an HTML page as a standalone object. Thus it can not only be included in any web-based instructional module but it can be simultaneously used by as many users as the server hosting it can support.

A third commonly used technology for implementing LOs is Flash™ movies. While there are striking similarities in the ways Flash movies and Java applets can be included in a web browser, they differ in the process of creation, resource utilization, and capabilities. Below is an example of embedding a Flash object in a browser,

```
<object classid="clsid:8AC840-044E-111-B39-
005F499D93"
                width="200" height="200">
                <param name="movie"
                value="http://www.capella.edu/objects/gravity.swf">
</object>
```

The object *gravity.swf* is accessed from the same repository as the applet in the previous example. While Java applets and Flash movies are both geared towards creating media-rich user experiences, applets are considerably harder to create and require higher expertise in computer programming. However they are particularly suited for applications which require intensive use of networking and implementation of complex algorithms. Flash movies are particularly strong in the area of animations and visual effects, and the way they can integrate many types of data including video, audio and hi resolution graphics.

The examples of LOs described above are by no means exhaustive of the topic. However, they do possess representative properties relevant to this discussion:

- They are self contained
- They can be stored in an independent repository
- They can be accessed over the Internet in a web browser
- They are architected so that data they processed is loaded from outside the object
- They are reusable
- They are scalable in terms on number of simultaneous users, amount of data processed, and length of use

Impact of LOs on Representative ODL Practices

Bennett and McGee (2005) survey the impact learning objects have on designing new models for distance education delivery and management. They propose that LOs can foster the development of more progressive course management systems (CMS), ones that move beyond the traditional paradigms of 'semester', 'course', 'credit', and 'textbook'. Underlying this thesis is the fact that while it is debatable whether LOs are the definitive next generation learning environments, they are changing the structure, the design, and the delivery of open and distance learning (ODL).

(ODL) has emerged as a concept in parallel to the growth and development of the Internet and its related technologies. When viewed as one application enabled by the Internet, ODL has fed of characteristics from several domains. First, the very architecture of the Internet enables access to information by learners, facilitators, and administrators asynchronously. Second, the concept of *open source software* has fostered open learning initiatives at the world's leading distance and traditional universities. Two such examples are The Massachusetts Institute of Technology and The Open University of the UK . Third, ODL providers cater to very diverse populations with a broad range of age, prior educational experience, financial capabilities, and geographic dispersion.

After an examination of various ODL environments the following core practices emerge as representative of the field, given their pervasiveness, popularity, and demand by consumers and providers of education. In a study commissioned by UNESCO, Jung (2005) identifies eight categories of ODL practices: "quality assurance, curriculum, policy and management, student services and tutoring, innovations, cost-savings, collaboration, and for-profit involvement." While not the only study on this topic, Jung has surveyed 13 "mega-universities" (some exceeding one million and two million students) in several countries in the Asia-Pacific region, where two thirds of the world population lives. Combined with the fact that the AP region is the fastest growing in term of ODL adoption

(Jung, 2005) it is fair to assume that these practices are representative for the field.

In the area of quality assurance ODL providers must face the challenges posed by designing instructional material that is grounded in current learning theory and practice. The technologies involved in online delivery of content pose an additional challenge similar to quality assurance required in any software engineering and technology sector: connection reliability, timely delivery, lossless transmission, and information accuracy. Digital LOs provide a significant advantage in this area given their self-contained and modular design. Software engineers need to maintain small chunks of code and an error in one module does not cause a cascading effect. In the case of XML objects, the simplicity of the code and the availability of data validators make it very easy to maintain XML object repositories. Given the prevalence of XML-based content management systems and XML-based authoring frameworks, one would expect to see an increased number of XML-based LOs. This expectation is also supported by the fact that the overhead associated with XML is simply text and all web browsers are capable of reading XML without the need for additional software. More complex objects, such as those written in Java or Flash, require longer development and debugging cycles. Thus they are somewhat less attractive for an ODL environment unless there is a committed effort industry-wide to create standards-based (e.g. SCORM) objects that are certified to be reliable, stable, and bug-free buy their developers.

Online curriculum designers must meet the same requirements as any education provider. However, not all classroom based curricula translate directly into a web-based medium. Furthermore, not all translate well into an open learning environment. ODL curriculum must cover defined competencies in a field while adapting the coverage depth of topics and their sequencing to the diversity of the student population and their isolated study environment. This area is one which benefits the most from the flexibility provided by digital LOs. The ability to mix and match objects from various sources and in various languages makes it possible for curriculum designers to plan highly adaptable course sequences. Furthermore, when competency requirements change it is easy to make granular and incremental changes and thus keep curricula continuously up to date. Arguably the ability to provide a customizable curriculum and courses is by far more significant than the ease of code maintenance. Such flexibility and sophistication is more readily achievable with more complex LOs, such as ones written in Java or Flash. The ability, for example of Java applets to communicate with objects across networks enables the creation of *ad-hoc federations of objects*, a concept increasingly popular in the computer programmers community.

Policy, management, student tutoring and services are less relevant to the discussion in this paper and thus not covered. It suffices to say that diversity, geographic dispersion, cultural and language differences account for the bulk of the factors that influence policy and services.

In the category of innovation, ODL is driven by the relentless innovation spurred by the Internet and its related technologies. The development, deployment, and maintenance of new software, networking protocols and interaction devices are often paced much faster than the development of instructional design practices and learning theory. Thus ODL providers must continuously adapt delivery methods to the increasing demands of the Internet savvy student population. Such practices risk sacrificing good pedagogy in favor to creating an image of a technologically advanced institution. The phenomenal growth and innovation associated with the Internet directly impact ODL, which after all relies on these technologies. The increased ubiquity of high speed networks, wired or wireless, on desktops as well as PDAs and mobile phones, create opportunity to interact with learning environments almost anytime, anywhere. Combined with the growing trend of being always online, there is an opportunity to provide accelerated learning programs. Whereas traditional instruction is based on weekly class meetings, ODL is delivered continuously. Busy, working adults, who form the vast majority of ODL students, are finding the ability to participate in online classes whenever there is a free moment very appealing. With the advent of Java-enabled smart phones and Wi-Fi, Java applet-based LOs can be designed to be cross-platform and self adaptable to the limitations of small screens. While not really a desktop replacement, the ability of small devices to deliver news, text messages, and financial data is easily ported to deliver educational content. It would be interesting to follow the impact of new technologies like streaming applications on ODL. For example, the ability to stream code similar to streaming video can open the door to rich applications, built with rich LOs, delivered on demand to any Internet-connected device. One development could be the placement on LO repositories onto media streaming servers networks (e.g. Akamai). Thus objects can be automatically delivered to learners even if they travel worldwide.

ODL presents an obvious economy of scale. Simply put, it doesn't take 1,000 times more resources to support 1,000 students than it takes to support one student. Thus the cost savings are evident. ODL, as mentioned earlier, is influenced by the open source software movement. In addition, several prominent universities like MIT and Carnegie Mellon are placing educational content (e.g. entire courses) online for free use. The combination of free or almost free software, scalability and partially free content are decisive in promoting cost savings for institutions as well as for learners. One of the major cost factors in software development is code maintenance and re-writes. Since each LO is a standalone, typically small chunk of code and data, the development and deployment cycles are fairly small and are measured in weeks. The relative ease of programming LOs enable setting policies of frequent updates, thus keeping LOs in line with demand and changing requirements. The modularity of LOs also means quick initial deployment and easy incremental updates. The server-based approach to LO delivery also means that educational modules need be updated only on few locations (and mirrors). For example portions of chapters in digital textbooks can be revised in the databases and the content can be delivered using XML templates to multiple destinations, all using the same source.

Collaboration in online environments is a natural activity for all Internet users. Chat, text messaging, email, tagging, and video conferencing are all tools that distance education has adopted. All being free, they make an even more appealing addition to ODL. Online collaboration tools are a perfect environment for implementing constructivist and social-constructivist learning environments. However, the impact of LOs in this area is minimal, if noticeable at all. The nature of ODL is such that learning activities are individual. Therefore the impact of LOs is felt mainly in those areas where the individual learner interacts with the educational content. Interaction among learners is not a function of content as much as it is a function of the learning environment, i.e. the technologies which enable communication, data exchange, and sharing resources. There is, however one potential area in which the use of LOs may impact collaboration: peer-to-peer networking. Akin to sharing music or books, online learners could also share LOs or even entire course packages. Judging from the success of technologies like BitTorrent™ or Napster™, one could envision a similar development aimed at sharing knowledge and education in addition to entertainment.

For-profit involvement is always a contentious issue in respect with higher education. In some countries higher education is free (to their citizens), while in other countries students pay high tuition rates. The Internet has no borders and by definition ODL is open to all. Thus providers must balance their financial needs with the mission of providing open education which is accessible to all students. Profiting from education is largely a macro-level business and political decision, outside of the scope of this discussion. From a technological standpoint LOs offer some unique opportunities on the micro level. Should an ODL provider choose to do so, it is possible to create a business model based on learners purchasing or leasing small educational modules (e.g. LOs) for a very small fee, say pennies a month. The granularity of information and the ability to track its use means that institutions can offer highly customized educational packages priced a la carte. The segmentation of educational content enabled by LOs enables the creation of multiple versions of course content, priced to reflect usage patterns and market demands.

A Model for a Personalized Learning Environment

E-Learning occurs in virtual space, without physical interaction with classmates and teachers (learning facilitators), which are the staples of traditional schools. The difference in approaches to learning can be accommodated and encouraged by learning environments which cater to these differences Danchak (2005). A few issues in this context are:

a. Individualized performance evaluation, in the absence of a comparison to peers may be biased. Grade normalization, a common practice among instructors, is impossible in a one-student "class".

b. E-Learning increases the opportunity for copyright infringement due to (still) naïve learner identification protocols. This issue is of particular importance when assessing performance in major course projects.

c. Typical work environments require teamwork and in-person attendance. It is unclear whether knowledge transfers into the learner's work environment in a different manner compared to a traditional face-to-face program.

d. Not all programs, in-class or online, produce competent graduates, ready to assume roles in their chosen profession. In part to blame are academic evaluation and assessment methods, which are often different than the ones employed by businesses.

This discrepancy is noted by Weller (2004) who found that "By using a learning-object approach, it is feasible to create courses on the fly that will be well suited to the individual learner....They will be better suited to learning within the workplace and are well suited to a just-in-time approach." According to Weller the personalization of eLearning is recommended by other research results. Lave and

Wagner claim in Weller (2004) that "while training company providers are also engaged in this reuse activity, they are aiming at what they perceive to be a much bigger market: content aggregation on the fly by individual learners or training providers." The increasingly popular SCORM approach to the design and delivery of eLearning is touted by the (US Army originated) ADL Initiative (2005) as ensuring "access to high-quality education and training materials that can be tailored to individual learners".

In view of the technical possibilities offered by learning objects and the advantages of addressing each learner's personal needs it is possible to envision a learning environment that offers self-adaptable, personalized lessons, personalized practice, personalized evaluation, and even a personalized academic degree. Along all stages of this program highly granular activity tracking can be implemented.

The following is an algorithm that prescribes how such a model can be implemented:

1. Learner takes an online multiple choice assessment test on the subject matter; the test results automatically place the learner in one of three categories: beginner, advanced, expert.
2. Learner takes a secondary assessment test to narrow the program of study (customized major).
3. A list of courses is generated, each with a list of competencies. A chronological program of study is also generated.

4. Learner enrolls in one or more courses as prescribed by the algorithm. The steps below are repeated for each course.

5. Initial set of lesson modules is generated, following the chronology established in Step 4.

6. The system chooses from a library of learning objects the ones necessary for each module: presentation LOs, practice LOs, assessment LOs, and feedback LOs.

7. At the end of each lesson, learner takes a short assessment test. The results decided whether any of the LOs in a lesson, throughout the course, need to be replaced.

8. The system adapts and modifies itself continuously thus creating a personalized course, with personalized lessons, practice, and assessment.

9. The system tracks learner activities at the LO level and generates continuous reports on usage and performance. This feedback can be used for manual auditing of system decisions and for improvement of decisions algorithms.

Evaluation of the Model

Upon exposing the concerns regarding knowledge transfer it is worth focusing now on how customized assessment methods can help identify learners' readiness for real world performance.

As far back as 14 years ago Lehman and Granger found that "Empire State College … specifically addresses the evaluation issues raised by an individualized educational program for adults. Empire State's program provides for an individually designed degree plan and learning contracts ... In a fundamental sense, an individualized educational program requires an individualized assessment strategy (Hodgkinson, 1975). Until recently however, individualized assessment seemed prohibitively difficult and expensive for most colleges." Lehman and Granger (1991) pointed out the same issue which researchers raised 15 years ago (for them) and 30 years ago for. It seems logical that this issue should be finally addressed within the context of the revolutionary approach to learning fostered by the Internet.

The preparation of learners for real life performance often involves the teaching of specific skills. The performance level required by these skills can only be achieved if the practice completely mimics the desired and result. A perfect match between web based training for work skills and a learner's personal goal is not guaranteed. However, a personalized approach to training can enable great progress towards an acceptable match. When there is no convergence between personal goals and personalized assessment, who can one test whether goals are being met?

Let us a look at scenarios that expand on this assertion. A student is enrolled in a Statistics class. The student is required to submit solutions to a series of problems involving the concept of normal distribution. Let us look at how different set of circumstances may affect the performance and evaluation of a particular student.

In one scenario the student A is enrolled in the class because it is required by the Educational Program he is in. The student must demonstrate the ability to solve specific problems involving normal distribution. A must demonstrate the ability to solve a system of linear equations. Student A hopes to excel in the class rather than just merely passing. In contrast, student B is enrolled in the class because her employer pays for it. If she passes the class, she will earn professional development points which will translate into a higher salary. Consequently student B is content to simply passing and can even afford to fail some exams. Student C is getting a degree in Statistics Education and hopes to become a Statistics teacher. For student C there are two requirements for passing the class: demonstration of problem solving ability as well as teaching ability. There is also a minimum grade requirement of 80%.

If the college offers one statistics class not all students' above-outlined requirements will be met. Education students could be offered a slightly different version of a Statistics class, which also teaches instruction delivery specific to Statistics. Other students only need to learn problem solving at the level relevant to their intended professional objectives. If all three students are enrolled in the same class, they will treat with varied degrees of interest and will express varied degrees of satisfaction. Why not design a personalized program that will address each student's specific needs and induce genuine enthusiasm for achieving the highest level of (personal) excellence?

The above example is obviously not unique to Statistics. It clearly demonstrates the value of customized student evaluation. E-Learning enables asynchronous activities which students can submit at their own pace. Online interactive sessions can be customized to individual objectives and requirements by customized academic programs. Students *A, B,* and *C* presented earlier would benefit from an ideal match between expectation, evaluation, and desired performance.

Student *A* may choose to log into additional modules available once basic performance levels have been reached. Being an Education major, student *A* is likely to be required to demonstrate an understanding of statistical principles and their applications in Educational research (for example). Student B is likely to choose the easiest, quickest path to a passing grade. Any attempt to present her with material "to expand her horizons" would be futile. Student *C* is likely to be asked to prepare a multimedia presentation that demonstrates teaching capabilities. It is also likely that student C would also be required to learn about instruction delivery as part of a customized Statistics class. Current technology from mainstream vendors like Macromedia (Flash, Dreamweaver), and implementation of Reusable Learning Objects allows the easy creation of a personalized learning and evaluation experience. Furthermore, students A, B, and C will be able to participate in the same class but evaluated differently.

This notion is supported by Rossman (2002), who states that "In time our mass-produced standard subject-matter tests would be replaced with individualized testing that adequately takes account of unique learning style, talents, opportunities, needs, handicaps, limitations diagnosis. At each periodic examination the questions and procedures should take account of the learning history of the individual, should propose programs for deficiencies and more."

E-Learning is flexible enough to accommodate to accommodate the level of individualism promoted here. Kashy found in Swan (2001) that "ongoing assessment of student performance linked to immediate feedback and individualized instruction supports learning."

While the idea of personalized assessment may be appealing to some, others may object on the grounds that it lacks a control mechanism – a way to compare a student performance with peers in a class. This might diminish the validity of a grade and might negatively impact how an entire (individualized) program is viewed.

In a research conducted at the University of Albany, Moore (2004) found that distance learning programs actually prefer the custom approach to delivery and assessment: "In the University of Albany's computer and media education courses, students participate in and learn to create lesson plans incorporating rubrics—not only do rubrics help assess student performance, by helping students focus on what matters in the course, they help refine the course and reduce questions... Michigan State University uses LON-CAPA, open-source freeware for assessment and content management, to obtain immediate, detailed feedback about online homework, which can be used to quickly adjust lectures, recitation sessions, and individual help to address learner needs."

Real life surrounds us with personalized experiences. It is only natural that education should be treated the same like, for example, financial matters, job responsibilities, interior design preferences, and clothing. The way learners and instructors interact is very personal. So are each individual's personal and professional goals. Furthermore, academic institutions issue diplomas to individuals and not to groups. It is only natural to add to this list an individualized assessment approach. This claim is supported by research results presented in Graves (2004) in which he states that "The instructor, working with any assistants who might be involved in the instructional process, can design strategies for individualized student interventions by using [...] continuous assessment strategies".

The nature of learning is such that it transforms people. Therefore not only assessment should be personalized, but it should adapt to developmental growth a student may experience during the course of studies In summary, the personal nature and force with which the Internet affects lifestyles, business and technology cannot be opposed by traditions in education.

Already at the forefront of an educational revolution, eLearning providers can stretch their lead over traditional institutions once again, as tradition tries to keep up with change. Research cited earlier in this paper indicates that both learners and their future employers support the drive towards personalized assessment. Some academic institutions were shown to have taken initial steps, some even 15 years ago. While traditional institutions still produce the Ford Model T equivalent of academic programs, online schools are moving towards the equivalent of build-your-car-a-la-carte-online approach. It is reasonable to assume that personalization will take root in academic programs across the board. Then there will be time for a new evolutionary development. Perhaps genetic engineering approach to customized abilities...

On Planning and Maintenance of Web Based Training Programs

The following is a plan for course testing, evaluation, and maintenance of WBT within a distance education program. At the core of the course testing there is an augmented heuristic evaluation based on Nielsen (2000) and my own practice. The plan consists of 5 steps as following:

Phase I: Testing

1. Preliminary step – define error severity ratings

(a) Establish a team of evaluators which consists of instructional designers, graphics designers, web developers, and usability testers. The team is lead by a Testing Manager.

(b) Define four types of problems (issues) the evaluators would look for. Use a scale from 1 to 4 to rank types of problems

1. **Cosmetic problem only**: need not be fixed unless extra time is available on project

2. **Minor problem**: fixing this should be given low priority

3. **Major problem:** important to fix, and should be given high priority

4. **Catastrophe**: imperative to fix this before course can be started

(c) Define a set of 10 heuristics based on Nielsen (2000)

2. **Problem location**

Each evaluator examines the WBT program from their own perspective and creates a list of problems found and their severity. Evaluators test the program in two different ways. One is "hunting" for problems in all areas, based on their expertise. The second is recording violation of Nielsen's 10 heuristics. Evaluators meet and discuss their findings. Each individual evaluator summarizes his or her suggestions for change.

3. **Assembling data**

(a) Quantitative measures

    1.   The Testing Manager compiles an aggregate list of all problems found by each evaluator. A table of overall unique problems is created, highlighting the number of unique errors.

    2.   How many errors did each evaluator find? A table summarizing the number of problems and severity reported by each evaluator is compiled. The table will inform of problems specific for one area (stemming from the different evaluation perspectives)

(b) Heuristic violation graph (see example below)

    1.   Make a bar chart to show number of violations per heuristic (x-axis represents heuristic, y-axis represents number of violations). A quick look at the chart will immediately indicate problematic areas and focus attention.

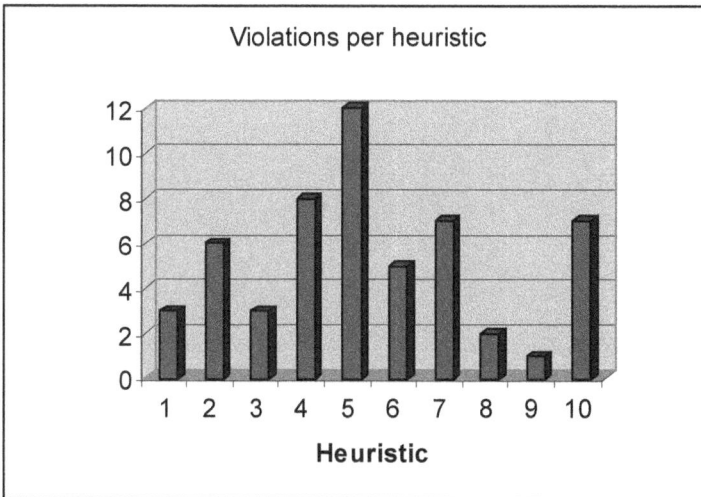

Violations per heuristic

2. List and describe trends as reflected from the chart.

(c) Severity proportion chart (see example below)
   1. Show the number of problems of each type that were found in a form of a pie chart. A high number of type 4 (the severest type) errors may trigger major changes for site, maybe complete redesign

Severity proportion chart

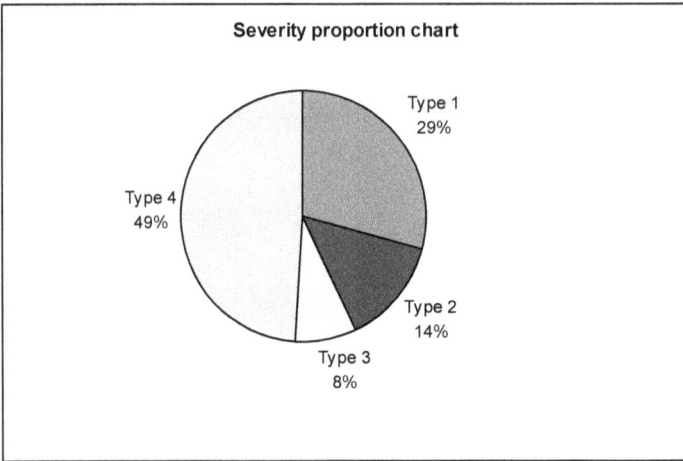

Type 1
29%

Type 4
49%

Type 2
14%

Type 3
8%

4. Thematic trends

(a) The testing Manager lists any thematic trends reflected by
aggregated problems sets (e.g. terminology, language,)

5. Putting it all together

(a) The Testing Manager summarizes the team's suggestions into
bullet points so that a clear set of objectives for improvement is
presented

(b) Cite specific instances and locations rather than general
concepts

(c) Make the list impossible to **not** understand

Phase II: Evaluation

The evaluation plan will be based on Kirkpatrick's four-step model, as described in Conrad (2000, p. 186). The four components of this model are *reaction, learning, behavior,* and *results.*

Step 1: Reaction – It is based on Kirkpatrick's notion that negative reaction by learners is an indicator of handicapped WBT program. The specific evaluation will consist of several administering surveys to students. The surveys will be administered in the middle and at the end of each course and then aggregate results and statistical analysis will be used to assess the learners' reaction to the WBT program as a whole. The following is an illustration of a survey administered to students:

Level of detail was appropriate	Strongly agree	Agree	Neutral	Disagree	Strongly disagree
Material was presented in an organized manner	Strongly agree	Agree	Neutral	Disagree	Strongly disagree
Lessons were interesting	Strongly agree	Agree	Neutral	Disagree	Strongly disagree
Material was consistent with industry requirements	Strongly agree	Agree	Neutral	Disagree	Strongly disagree
Information was presented in a clear manner	Strongly agree	Agree	Neutral	Disagree	Strongly disagree
A roadmap of the course content was presented	Strongly agree	Agree	Neutral	Disagree	Strongly disagree
Instruction was responsive to feedback on pace and navigation	Strongly agree	Agree	Neutral	Disagree	Strongly disagree
The user interface was effective	Strongly agree	Agree	Neutral	Disagree	Strongly disagree
The user interface was easy to use	Strongly agree	Agree	Neutral	Disagree	Strongly disagree

Resources were easily accessible	Strongly agree	Agree	Neutral	Disagree	Strongly disagree
System can save status - learner can exit and return to the same location	Strongly agree	Agree	Neutral	Disagree	Strongly disagree
Rate your prior experience with WBT	WBT developer	Very experienced	Experienced	Somewhat experienced	None

Upon completion of the surveys in each class, the data will be aggregated using the form below. The aggregate results will quickly indicate areas that need further development or remediation.

METRIC	Strongly agree %	Agree %	Neutral %	Disagree %	Strongly disagree %
Level of detail was appropriate					
Material was presented in an organized manner					
Lessons were interesting					
Material was consistent with industry					

requirements					
Information was presented in a clear manner					
A roadmap of the course content was presented					
Instruction was responsive to feedback on pace and navigation					
The user interface was effective					
The user interface was easy to use					
Resources were easily accessible					
System can save status - learner can exit and return to the same location					
Rate your prior experience with WBT					

Upon completion of this phase, a Reaction Survey Report will be prepared and submitted to the WBT Maintenance Program Manager.

Step 2: Learning – It is based on Armstrong (2004) which recommends both formative and summative evaluation of mastery of learning objectives. Hanlis describes in Armstrong (2004, p.43) a process of administering mid-course and end-of-course evaluations and final exams which are specifically designed to assess the following aspects of learning:

- Were instructional objectives suitable?
- Was the subject content appropriate?
- How did learning methods influence student performance?
- How do LMS-related functions correlate to demonstrated learner performance?
- How did communication affect learning?
- How did actual student performance compare to the expected?

The above are guidelines which point to information that can be extracted directly from analyzing results of student performance in homework assignments, projects, exams, and term papers. It implies that the WBT system employs an adequate mechanism for tracking metrics required by such an analysis. For example: time spent online (broken down by activities), time lapse between beginning and submission of assignments, and grading scales normalization tools.

Upon completion of this phase, a Learning Survey Report will be prepared and submitted to the WBT Maintenance Program Manager.

Step 3: Behavior – It is suggested by Conrad's (2000, p. 190) notion that an important attribute of a successful WBT program (like any educational program) is the transfer of knowledge into the workplace. An excellent treatment of this topic is presented by Clark (2003).

Clark (2003) distinguishes between three types of transfer: near, moderate, and far. On page 148 she presents two teaching strategies for near-transfer performance: training wheels or scaffolding and part task drill and practice.

The first strategy is based on providing external support to learners until they are capable to perform on their own. This can be accomplished by providing guiding templates and hints for example. In a computer programming class, the instructor may implement scaffolding strategies by providing skeletons of computer programs, to which students can gradually add their own code. In the workplace, employees are asked to create a computer program entirely on their own. Success in such endeavors is measured by surveying employers.

The second strategy is more applicable to performance oriented skills such as essay writing, painting, or driving a car. The key element in this approach (Clark 2003, p. 149) is to break a task into sub-task and practice each one separately, until the student can gradually move towards performing the entire task. Eventually the employees are expected to complete a task from start to finish. Successful completion can be documented and reported by employers to the employee's educational institution.

Moderate transfer is prevalent in work environments where employees are required to perform a skill across different situations and scenarios. One way to bring about this type of transfer is to move from specific to general procedures (Clark 2003, p. 150). For example, employees may be shown in a lab the specific steps of how to accurately measure the temperature of a liquid inside a container. Later on they may be asked to inspect different facilities in a chemical plant and test the temperature of liquids in various types and sizes of containers.

While transitioning from one system or environment to another, one is likely to improve performance if in addition to learning how to execute a task one also learns why a given system behaves or reacts the way it does (Clark 2003, p. 151). The working principles of a system or a machine are unlikely to change over a short period of time. Thus it is beneficial to promote understanding of operating principles rather than memorizing a particular implementation sequence. For example, if one understands the steps to follow in order to read schematics of electrical circuits for a simple radio, one could also read schematics for TV sets and DVD players.

Far transfer is the most challenging form of transfer since it requires the learner to understand and/or interact with new situations by making analogies or extrapolating (to) situations previously experienced in a class or lab. The process of guided discovery seems to be suitable for accomplishing far transfer because it provides learners with the opportunity to venture into new areas while someone else points out similarities and analogies to situations and systems which are already known. Performance by employees of research companies is an excellent indicator of the success of the WBT program the employees have participated in.

Upon completion of this phase, a Behavior Survey Report will be prepared and submitted to the WBT Maintenance Program Manager.

Step 4: Results – It is based on Johnson (2005) from the University of South Alabama, who teaches extensively about Kirkpatrick's four-level model. The results level of Kirkpatrick's model refers to the bottom line performance of the learner-employee in the workplace. In other words, it is an assessment of the employer of the worthiness of training, in terms of ROI (return on investment). From the employer's viewpoint outcomes are changes in financial outcomes or changes in variables that should affect financial outcomes in the future.

Johnson (2005) proposes the following outcomes which can be measured through post-training surveys sent to employers.

Metric	Value prior to training	Value post training	Desired value	Bottom line: was it worth it?

Improved quality of work				
Higher productivity.				
Reduction in turnover				
Reduction in scrap rate (i.e., less wasted resources				
Improved quality of work life				
Improved human relations (e.g., improved vertical and horizontal				
Fewer grievances				
Lower absenteeism				
Higher worker morale.				
Fewer accidents				
Greater job satisfaction				
Increased profits.				

Upon completion of this phase, a Results Survey Report will be prepared and submitted to the WBT Maintenance Program Manager. The report will include detailed recommendations based on aggregate feedback from employers.

Phase III: Maintenance

The maintenance process of a WBT program is cyclical. It consists primarily of repeating phases I and II described above while correcting problems uncovered at each phase. This process is ongoing throughout the lifetime of a WBT program. Maintenance is not a standalone phase, which occurs independently of other phases. Rather it is intertwined within testing and evaluation (Conrad, 2000, p. 191).

In general terms maintenances consists of implementing changes at the end of the testing and evaluation phase. A recommended maintenance schedule is presented below:

Post-testing maintenance:

- Review heuristic violation graph and make a list of priorities for change
- Review the severity proportion chart and list all the problems which need to be fixed, ranked in order of priority based on severity.
- Review the comments and recommendations made by the Testing Manager and schedule implementations of specific changes accordingly

Post-evaluation maintenance:

- Review the Reaction Survey Report and list changes to be made. Assign higher priority to issues rated as "Strongly disagree"
- Review the Learning Survey Report and list changes to be made in order to address issues identified as hindering learning.
- Review the Behavior Survey Report and list changes to be made in order to increase near, moderate, and

far transfer. Implement recommendations made in the report.

- Review the Results Survey Report and list changes to be made in order to respond to feedback provided by employers.

The best way to describe the entire plan for WBT evaluation is to follow the flowchart below:

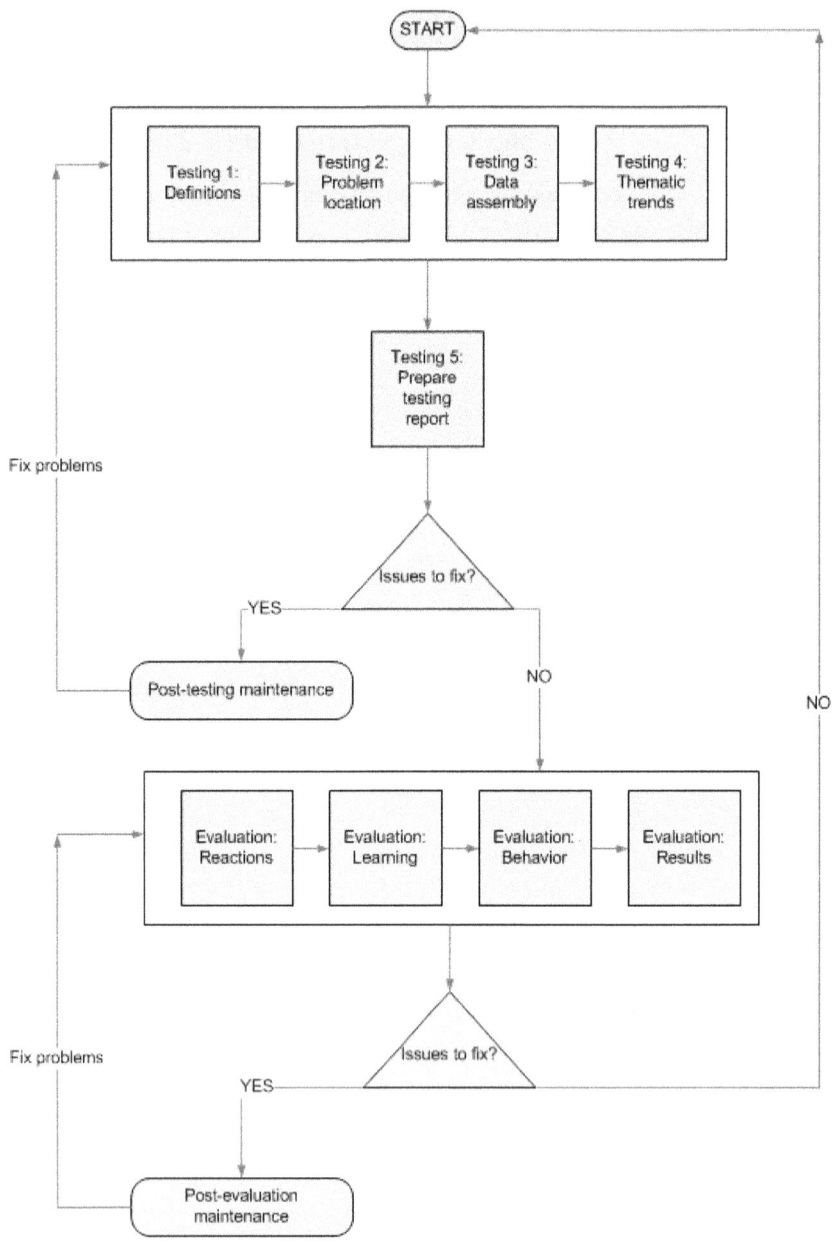

START

Testing 1: Definitions → Testing 2: Problem location → Testing 3: Data assembly → Testing 4: Thematic trends

Testing 5: Prepare testing report

Fix problems

Issues to fix?

YES

NO

Post-testing maintenance

NO

Evaluation: Reactions → Evaluation: Learning → Evaluation: Behavior → Evaluation: Results

Fix problems

Issues to fix?

YES

Post-evaluation maintenance

Objectives and Strategies for a Distance Education Program

A distance education program must provide learners the same educational experience, or superior, as a traditional classroom one. A study conducted by New River Community College, NRCC (2005) found that most distance learners are professional adults in their 30s, full-time employed, with families, with some college experience, and could attend traditional classes. Therefore any distance education program must set objectives that cater to the specific needs of this population.

Objectives for a distance education program

The objectives of successful distance learning program can be grouped into three categories: academic, professional, and social.

Academic objectives relate mastery of skills and competencies required by a program. In the spirit of Conrad (2000, p. 87) important academic objectives are:

- The skills and knowledge acquired by learners should parallel or exceed the requirements outlined by the program.
- In spite of the *distance* element in learning the methods of delivery must provide learners with an experience similar to the one they are expected to encounter in typical applications of the skill set.

- The program must enable students to perform at levels similar or better than traditional face to face education.
- The program must provide access to virtual tools like libraries, research facilities, and communication with peers and instructors that make the learning environment similar or superior to any other environment
- Rigorous user authentication methods must ensure that work submitted online is indeed created by those who claim they did; this is imperative to combat those who are skeptical about the validity of distance learning achievements.

In the context of a single course academic objectives will pertain more to accommodating different learning styles, format of presentation (e.g. simulations, video clips), and interaction between instructor and learner (Conrad, 2000, p.94). Professional objectives refer to the integration of learning activities in the life of a professional adult. Specific examples of such objectives are:

- Access to the LMS should be available from any Internet-connected device, to eliminate potential waste of time finding a suitable machine or disrupting the learner's work schedule.
- The quality of and diligence of the program must be commensurate with corporate employers in order to ensure recognition, qualifications, and accreditation.
- The program must provide enough flexibility to accommodate the variety of professional constraints imposed on the learner (e.g. schedule, pace, cost)

These objectives will remain the same in the context of individual courses. Social objectives of a distance learning program refer largely to the integration of the learner's academic and social lives. Considering the profile of a typical distance learner describe above, some important social objectives are:

- Course load should balance the priority learners assign to their family and social activities with the need to complete a program within a reasonable time frame.

- The LMS should provide a section in which learners can socialize and provide the "water cooler" experience available in traditional colleges.

- The program must be mindful of current skepticism about the quality of distance education and provide verifiable qualitative and quantitative indicators that would promote a positive social image of distance learners (Jones et al, 2002). These objectives will remain the same in the context of individual courses.

Measurement strategies

Generally objectives should be defined in quantitative, behavioral terms. For example the achievement of academic objectives can be measured by conducting periodic evaluations (online tests) in which learners must pass a predetermined threshold (passing grade). This could be different than the individual course threshold. For example successful course completion could require 70% success, but program completion could require 80%. Thus mediocre, passing performance in a course will not be sufficient for overall proof of competency.

The assessment of professional objectives should involve both learners and employers. Online surveys measuring changes in the learner's work performance, attitudes, and competence should be separately administered to learners and employers. The aggregate results, combined with individual analysis should provide a realistic measure of success.

Measurement of social objectives can be very subjective and dependant on individual circumstances. A useful strategy would be to create a set of learner expectations and compare to actual feedback at the beginning, middle and end of a program or individual course.

All above mentioned strategies should accommodate variations and adaptations. A distance learning program which serves a very diverse population will have a hard time devising generic evaluation methods. In such a situation the program might find it useful to include detailed profiling data in each quantitative and qualitative evaluation. To the extent that these methods do not infringe on personal privacy regulations, they can enable the extraction of useful information otherwise not available. For example a survey of online Algebra students in an international distance learning program may reveal that students from one particular country are better prepared than other students and should be enrolled in a more advanced class. Jones et al (2002) found for example that females score better than males in distance education programs.

Part 3

Technology and Learning

Computer Games as an Instructional Tool

This essay discusses the development of research questions
for a study on the use of computer games in college instruction

Introduction

Survey data suggests that art students are bored with classes not directly related to their core (design, graphics, and animation). The challenge is to teach left-brain skills to right-brain students. It is not known whether the use of computer games as a learning environment can be an effective learning tool for digital art students.

This paper examines some of the findings in the literature pertaining to the role of computer and video games in instruction. The discussion of these findings will be ultimately used to help define research questions for a doctoral dissertation. All studies cited examine current trends in the pervasiveness of video games for recreation by children and adults alike. Current college students, especially ones enrolled in digital arts related disciplines, are avid gamers. Many studies suggest that students' familiarity with video games can be harnessed for the creation of more efficient learning environments or such that overcome existing barrier to learning.

Survey of Literature

Carstens and Beck (2005) cite research evidence that shows the strong impact video games have on children during the growth period and maturation of their neural pathways.

The current student generation is one accustomed to spend many hours each week interacting with intricate video games. Carstens and Beck recommend that the "gamer generation" of students be taught in ways similar to the games they play: little formal instruction, many trial and error exercises, multi-user gaming environments, and risk taking in a safe environment. Digital Art students are almost all gamers. Consequently it is important to investigate how (educational) computer games can be used as learning environments in Art curricula.

Corbit (2005) cites a report by EDUCAUSE stating that "games represent active, immersive learning environments where users integrate information to solve a problem. Learning in this manner incorporates discovery, analysis, interpretation, and performance as well as physical and mental activity." Corbit (2005) also describes research conducted at Cornell University, entitled SciCenter, an immersive, virtual reality learning environment used to simulate hands-on science experiments. While these examples are not specifically applied to digital art disciplines they raise the need to answer questions regarding their particular suitability to digital art majors. A potential such research question is "Do digital art students perform better in Math classes when they use learning environments modeled after video games?"

DeKanter (2005) surveys the merits of constructivist learning environments. This approach is already implemented in digital arts classes, in which students are often collaborating on projects. In contrast, the study of Math, for example, is typically more structured, less group oriented, and drill driven. Thus it is no surprise that digital art majors perceive it as a foreign entity, outside the scope and purpose of their core curriculum. Resistance to Math and Computer Programming classes can be dampened (DeKanter, 2005) by embracing video games as an integral part of modern pedagogy. DeKanter further strengthens his claim by citing numerous initiatives in creating video game-based learning environments that teach the "how" not only the "what". Thus students are able to detach from their natural animosity towards a topic and embrace it as part of the digital culture already familiar to them. DeKanter's view is supported by Carstens and Beck (2005), which state that gamers strive more than non-gamers to succeed as long as the goal has meaning to them. Just like video games present increased levels of difficulty as the game progresses, Math and Science instructional objectives can be attained using a game-like approach to multi-level discovery. An interesting research question would therefore be "Are gamers more motivated to learn Math and Science if it is presented in the form of a multilevel immersive video game?"

Kirkley and Kirkley (2005) offer their support for a constructivist approach to learning. They state that next generation learning environments are perfectly matching technological capabilities and possibilities with their audience and its characteristics. While they do not explicitly address art students as the target audience, their argument is further strengthen by the predominance of a gaming culture among such students. Kirkley and Kirkley point out that current instructional design methodology does not adequately prescribe how to incorporate virtual reality and immersive games within an instructional environment. In this context they describe a tool, IIPI CREATE, which allows instructional designers to merge the process of creating a game with developing activities to support specific instructional objectives. IIPI CREATE enables the creation of media rich, interactive, immersive, educational learning environments.

Kelly (2005) reminds us that in 1990, presidents Bush and Clinton started an initiative to make US students first in the world in Math and Science by 2000. In 2000 and 2003, US students were still ranked 22 among 27 industrialized nations. This finding contrasts with the technological advancements and innovations in the US during the same period. Kelly (2005) found that gamers spend hundreds of hours learning new weapon systems that help them win a video game. On the other hand they spend very little time trying to solve a Math problem in their homework. Such contrast amounts to an open invitation for researchers and game developers to find ways to bring the same enthusiasm gamers to learning "boring" topics like Algebra. Another research question stems from this call, one which supports those presented earlier in this paper: "How do games act as a motivational factor in learning Math and Science?" Children always used to play with toys. However, modern toys, embodied by immersive videogames, are played by adults of all ages. Their extent is so large that corporations and the military are using them to simulate realistic processes, procedures and events. Paradoxically, the current generation of students is accustomed to spending hours on digital simulations at home and is likely to encounter them in the workplace, but not while in college. This paradox is further emphasized by digital art majors who are trained precisely in creating video games. Kelly's findings provide additional backing to the need for investigating how video games can be designed to serve as learning environments.

Squire et al (2005) describe their study into the role of multiplayer computer games in enabling students to achieve "digital literacy". A very important finding in this study is the suggestion that "expert strategy simulation game knowledge is a flexible, systemic level understanding of a game system rather than a simple heuristic understanding." One implication of such finding is that certain subjects are not inherently difficult and they can be overcome by changing the approach to learning. This is particularly important in the case of (digital) art students who often resent learning topics outside their core curriculum. Squire et al (2005) also point out that while game-like learning environments are not guaranteed to improve literacy in the traditional sense, they help students develop literacy skills required by the digital age. They also recommend that further research be conducted to assess overall improvement in academic performance of students engaged in digital game-based learning.

Lim, Nonis, and Hedberg (2006) explore the use of 3D simulations of science experiments. Their findings are consistent with the ones presented above by DeKanter (2005) and Squire et al (2005). Lim, Norris, and Hedberg found that students engaged in multi-user virtual environment are likely to exchange knowledge, are motivated to learn, and consider learning activities to be fun and exciting. Given that digital art students are interacting daily with such environments, both as users and as developers, they are expected to have a natural affinity for them. According to Lim, Norris, and Hedberg (2006) 3D educational gaming environments succeed in engaging all players (students) in the learning activity. They encourage learning through discovery within a constructivist framework.

Standen and Brown (2005) examine a different area of the use of virtual reality (VR) based learning environments. Their study focuses on people with intellectual disabilities. By extension, one could describe any person's difficulty with a particular subject matter as intellectual disability. Standen and Brown found that VR enhances social and cognitive skills while avoiding lack of patience and frustration human teachers sometimes display. While not prescriptive in its nature, the findings of Standen and Brown (2005) help broaden the discussion on potential uses of VR as an instructional medium. Such a discussion can help narrow the focus of research questions presented earlier. For example, "What are the main characteristics of a VR learning environment aimed at teaching Project Management to Photography majors?"

Simson (2005) presents several statistic indicators that can contribute towards assessing the benefits of incorporating digital games in instruction. She cites a 2004 survey by the Entertainment Software Association which found that 60% of Americans play interactive games on a regular basis. Simson cites a report by Woodward & Gridina according to which children aged 2-17 spend 6.5 hours a day in front of an electronic screen: television, video game, or computer. Another report cited by Simson, Wilkens (2004), found in a survey of 27 university campuses, 100% of students played video games on computers or consoles. Against the background of these statistics, Simson (2005) discusses the difficult position teachers find themselves in as they feel they no longer control the pace of learning and the topic of interests of their students. This suggestion warrants further investigation into the potential of video game –based instruction to return the teachers to "the driving seat" of the educational agenda. Simson calls for teachers to embrace video games as a means for improving communication with their students. Finally, Simson suggests that given their familiarity with videogames, students are likely to feel more confident and safe in demonstrating their skills.

In contrast to some of the views presented in this paper, Paras and Bizzocchi (2005) caution against excessive reliance of games as instructional tools. Their main concern is the lack of reflection during gaming activities. Paras and Bizzocchi point out that reflection is an essential component of learning. Fast pace (video) games, while highly motivating and engaging, do not provide for reflection time. Rather they encourage player to use "brute force", try all venues until success, instead of thinking and finding the smartest (or shortest) path to success. Paras and Bizzocchi agree to all views presented by other studies in this paper, but they add their reservations about immersive games. While found to produce positive academic results, immersive video games risk showing students a distorted reality, giving them a false impression about the pace and processes they are likely to encounter in the real world.

Summary

The research surveyed in this paper is certainly not exhaustive, but it provides a good starting point towards defining research questions regarding the use of games as instructional tools, particularly for (digital) art students. All findings presented here seem to support the following views:

    a.   There is a need to investigate the use of games in instruction

    b.   (Video) games provide a constructivist learning environment

    c.   The current student generation views games as an integral part of their daily activities

    d.   Video games can improve academic achievement in certain areas

    e.   Video games are ubiquitous everywhere except in the classroom

These findings suggest several research questions worthy of treatment in a doctoral thesis. For example:

- Can games be an effective learning tool for digital art students?

- Is there a correlation between success in winning a computer game and academic success when using games as instructional tools?

- How can current instructional design methodologies be adapted to support immersive game-based learning environments?

- Do video games induce increased motivation of art students for studying subjects outside their core curriculum?

These questions and the ones presented throughout this paper could easily form the basis for defining a research question in a doctoral dissertation.

Communities of Online Gamers as a Learning Environment

Background

Art students are challenged by topics outside their major, for example Algebra and Computer programming. As an instructor at The Art Institute of Phoenix, I teach students enrolled in Digital Arts disciplines like Game Art & Design, Visual & Game Programming, and Interactive Media Design. Most of these students cannot sit in class without an iPod, have Internet-enabled mobile phones, own several Internet domains, and spend several hours a day playing video games, creating digital art for video games, or programming video games. They form gaming communities which play around the clock, even during class, and in some instances even during the final exam (for relaxation). These are not typical students found at "ordinary institutions". They are fantastic artists and technology enthusiasts. But, they dread Math and Science and hence score very low in these topics. The development of learning communities studying topics in exact sciences, which are particularly suitable for digital art students , is a challenging and rewarding task. This paper examines the reasoning behind developing educational activities based on multiplayer video games and simulations to aid this particular category of learners (art students) in tackling what is commonly referred to as "left brain" skills.

There are numerous examples of research that support a game-based approach to education. Some are discussed in this paper. Computer games are not only the realm of children nor are they limited to recreational activities. Given the ubiquity of online games it is worth exploring how to employ them in the teaching of Mathematical and Science concepts. Digital art students constitute a large percentage of the community of game developers. They are players, designers, critics, and up-to-date with the latest developments. It is only natural, therefore, to utilize this familiar environment as an educational tool for this particular student population.

Suggestions from Current Research

Computer games are the antithesis of structured activities. As such, they support a social constructivist approach to teaching and learning (DeKanter 2005). (Social) constructivism is the approach of choice in Art departments and it is suitable to students with artistic inclinations. Engineering students are more accustomed to structured instruction, befitting the engineering processes. Multiplayer video games can bridge the apparent conflict between subject matters that lend themselves to a predominantly structured approach and the preference to teach these subjects in a predominantly unstructured manner (DeKanter, 2005). Apple Computer Corporation is running a media campaign promoting a "digital lifestyle" – online access and sharing of digital media among like-minded individuals. There are few groups with which this resonates better than Digital Art students. DeKanter suggests that a digital lifestyle approach should be adopted for instruction. This would increase students' motivation and be in synchronization with the way young minds are being asked to think today. If 50 years ago students dreaded boring Math homework, is there any reason they would like it more today when they know how education can be presented in a fun and engaging way? DeKanter, as well as Carstens & Beck (2005), found that gamers succeed because games define objectives very well. In fact, Carstens & Beck found that defining objectives is so important that it affects the successful navigation of a difficult game. These findings alone should suggest interesting analogies between academic success and winning games. This is another validation of the notion that game-based instruction is a worthwhile topic for academic investigation. Multiplayer online games bring together a community focused on a common goal. However, while each player is set on individual gain (winning) unlimited rounds of the (often addictive) game offer an opportunity for each individual (or team) to ultimately win.

Today's children develop cognitive skills under heavy influence of electronic computer games (Carstens & Beck 2005). Thus they grow accustomed to interacting with a digital medium. The current generation of college students is the first to have matured with a gaming. Carstens & Beck found benefits in adopting a game-like experience to instruction, one in which students would be very comfortable with. Classroom instruction should use such practices like open dialogue, less structured instruction, learning through discovery, and encourage experimentation so that the "gamer generation" of students would be taught in ways similar to the games they play: little formal instruction, many trial and error exercises, multi-user gaming environments, and risk taking in a safe environment. Carstens & Beck's findings suggest that the transition from gaming as recreation to gaming as learning will resonate well Digital Art students.

Corbit (2005) support Carstens & Beck's findings entirely. Furthermore, Corbit suggest that the gaming experience should be immersive and users (i.e. learners) with only the game resources within the game to discover the solution to a problem. Such type of activity develops learners' cognitive and analytical skills. Several prominent institutions, such as Cornell University have explored the use of immersive gaming in science teaching (Corbit 2005). Given the dominant role video games play in the life of digital art students one should at least ponder at the notion that such students will show less resistance to topics like Math, if presented in the form of modern, interactive, multi-user games.

Similar to science literacy and numeracy, the digital world that is integral part of students' lives requires what Squire et al (2005) call "digital literacy". They found that gaming teaches higher order skills, similar to the ones required by academic learning. While thinking about winning strategies for games, players also develop generic strategic thinking skills. They also learn how to collaborate in groups and balance individual achievement with ream achievement. One implication of such finding is that certain subjects are not inherently difficult and they can be overcome by changing the approach to learning. This is particularly important in the case of Digital Arts students who often resent learning topics outside their core curriculum. Squire et al (2005) also point out that while game-like learning environments are not guaranteed to improve literacy in the traditional sense, they help students develop literacy skills required by the digital age. They also recommend that further research be conducted to assess overall improvement in academic performance of students engaged in digital game-based learning.

Another form of multi-player games, virtual reality science simulations, has been investigated by Lim, Nonis, and Hedberg (2006). Their findings are consistent with the ones presented above by DeKanter (2005) and Squire et al (2005). Lim, Norris, and Hedberg found that students engaged in a multi-user virtual environment are likely to exchange knowledge, are motivated to learn, and consider learning activities to be fun and exciting. Given that Digital Arts students are interacting daily with such environments, both as users and as developers, they are expected to have a natural affinity for them. According to Lim, Norris, and Hedberg (2006) 3D educational gaming environments succeed in engaging all players (students) in the learning activity. They encourage learning through discovery within a constructivist framework.

Kirkley and Kirkley (2005) offer their support for a constructivist approach to learning. They state that next generation group learning environments are perfectly matching technological capabilities and possibilities with their audience and its characteristics. While they do not explicitly address art students as the target audience, their argument is further strengthen by the predominance of a gaming culture among such students. Kirkley and Kirkley point out that current instructional design methodology does not adequately prescribe how to incorporate virtual reality and immersive games within a classroom instructional environment. In this context they describe a tool, IIPI CREATE, which allows instructional designers to merge the process of creating a game with developing online group activities to support specific instructional objectives. IIPI CREATE enables the creation of media rich, interactive, immersive, educational learning environments in which virtual learning teams can collaborate.

Kelly (2005) reminds us that in 1990, presidents Bush and Clinton started an initiative to for US students to become first in the world in Math and Science by 2000. In 2000 and 2003, US students were still ranked 22 among 27 industrialized nations. This finding contrasts with the technological advancements and innovations in the US during the same period. Kelly (2005) found that gamers spend hundreds of hours learning from each other new weapon systems that help them win a video game. On the other hand they spend very little time trying to solve a Math problem in their homework. Such contrast amounts to an open invitation for researchers and game developers to find ways to bring the same enthusiasm to learning "boring" topics like Algebra. It is worth investigating whether multiplayer video games act as a motivational factor in learning Math and Science. Children always used to play with toys. However, modern toys, embodied by immersive videogames, are played by adults of all ages. Their extent is so large that corporations and the military are using them to simulate realistic processes, procedures and events and for improving team collaboration. The current generation of students is accustomed to spending hours on digital simulations at home and are likely to encounter them in the workplace, but paradoxically, not while in college, at least not as an instructional medium. This paradox is further emphasized by digital art majors who are trained precisely in creating video games. They are exposed to the potential but their colleges do not harness it.

Standen and Brown (2005) examine a different area of the use of virtual reality (VR) based learning environments. Their study focuses on people with intellectual disabilities. For the purpose of illustrative exaggeration, one could describe any person's difficulty with a particular subject matter as intellectual disability. Standen and Brown found that VR enhances social and cognitive skills while avoiding lack of patience and frustration human teachers sometimes display. The comfort of online anonymity allows one to highlight strengths and hide deficiencies, those enabling the participation in select (gamer) groups otherwise not accessible. While not prescriptive in its nature, the findings of Standen and Brown (2005) help broaden the discussion on potential uses of VR as an instructional medium.

Simson (2005) presents several statistic indicators that can contribute towards assessing the benefits of incorporating multiplayer, team-based, digital games in instruction. She cites a 2004 survey by the Entertainment Software Association which found that 60% of Americans play interactive games on a regular basis. Simson cites a report by Woodward & Gridina according to which children aged 2-17 spend 6.5 hours a day in front of an electronic screen: television, video game, or computer. Another report cited by Simson, Wilkens (2004), found in a survey of 27 university campuses, 100% of students played video games on computers or consoles. Against the background of these statistics, Simson (2005) discusses the difficult position teachers find themselves in as they feel they no longer control the pace of learning and the topic of interests of their students. This suggestion warrants further investigation into the potential of video game–based instruction to return the teachers to "the driving seat" of the educational agenda. Simson calls for teachers to embrace video games as a means for improving communication with their students. Finally, Simson suggests that given their familiarity with videogames, students are likely to feel more confident and safe in demonstrating their skills, particularly in online games.

In contrast to some of the views presented in this paper, Paras and Bizzocchi (2005) caution against excessive reliance of games as instructional tools. Their main concern is the lack of reflection during gaming activities. Paras and Bizzocchi point out that reflection is an essential component of learning. Fast pace video games, while highly motivating and engaging, do not provide for reflection time. Rather they encourage player to use "brute force", try all venues until success, instead of thinking and finding the smartest (or shortest) path to success. Paras and Bizzocchi agree to most views presented by other studies mentioned in this paper, but they add their reservations about immersive games. While found to produce positive academic results, immersive video games risk showing students a distorted reality, giving them a false impression about the pace and processes they are likely to encounter in the real world.

Conclusion

The current generation of students is the first to not know a world without the Internet. They are accustomed to multitasking, hyper-linking, cannot live without iPods, SMS, web-enabled cell phones, blogs, TiVO, Xbox, GPS, etc. In short, anything lacking an electronic gadgetry dimension is considered archaic. Cosmetic changes in instruction, like learner-centered learning, distance education, web-based and multimedia-based content cannot hide the fact that instruction is still based on a teacher presenting materials, grading exams and papers, and assigning grades at the end of the semester. Digital Art students and faculty are perfectly suited to experiment with an innovative approach, extending classroom interaction to multi=player gaming activities. This would usher a transformation of the educational system and elevate it to the status of relevancy it deserves. Cell phones have become full-fledged Internet connected multimedia devices. So has television and not to mention the personal computer. It seems that everything around us beeps, sings, plays video, and automates something. A similar "mutation" in college education, face-to-face or online seems warranted. A mutation that will send the message that learning, particularly that which involves Math and Science is as essential as entertainment. The same technologies that get millions of adults addicted to shooting virtual space aliens can be used to teach Algebra, Calculus, History, and Social Science. We are still in a position to shape the development of game-based college instruction for those students who can benefit from it. If we let one more generation slip by before education becomes digitized, we risk letting the gaming industry fill in the void and create "educational" material based on a recreational view of the world.

Application of Evaluative Standards to Instructional Media Projects with Examples in Dreamweaver™ and Flash™

During the past two decades much research in educational psychology has been devoted to the understanding of cognitive processes that govern human learning. This essay describes some of the findings of this research and their implications in the design of instructional media projects. The connection between educational theory and technical implementation is established, as well as description of specific examples one could implement using Dreamweaver and Flash. The ultimate purpose of this essay is to provide a partial but essential set of guidelines to developers in an effort to encourage the application of learning theory in instructional design.

Evaluative Standards

The ultimate objective of instruction is that learners acquire knowledge and that the knowledge is transferred outside the classroom. Consequently instructional media projects for education must take into consideration human cognitive processes. Successful learning environments support cognitive learning processes which bring about effective professional performance. In order for an instructional program to succeed it must demonstrate the capability of transforming sensory data into retrievable knowledge in long-term memory (Clark, 2003, p.27). The following section describes 10 evaluative standards that will allow you to assess the soundness of the cognitive basis of the design of instructional media projects for education.

Standard 1: Managing Attention

It is hard to rank the evaluative standards discussed here in order of importance. However, it is fair to assume that managing attention is the key entry point into any educational program. How can learners acquire new knowledge if they are not listening, reading, or viewing? Clark (2003, p. 65) discusses three techniques for optimizing attention in a classroom: manage the physical environment, manage fatigue, and promote accountability and engagement.

Instructional media projects can be easily designed to accommodate all three techniques, with various levels of sophistication. Unlike textbooks, (online) media rich learning environments can be customized to the needs of various learner populations. Similar content can be presented using different examples, different levels of difficulty and over variable lesson durations. A rigid physical environment can become a dynamic virtual one, which preserves all the core features and attributes of the former without the handicap of "one size fits all" approach.

Since distance learning consists largely of asynchronous activities, managing fatigue takes a bit of a different meaning. It is more a pedagogical concept than a technological one. Fatigue can be monitored and addressed by varying the length and frequency of assignments. The absence of regularly scheduled live lectures allows learners to view recorded presentations at their own pace.

The promotion of accountability can be accomplished in multiple ways. A popular practice in distance learning programs is teamwork, in which members share responsibilities for projects and are held equally accountable for the team performance. My experience at Capella University and the University of Phoenix Online are a good indicator of this practice.

The actual implementation of attention management tools in an instructional media project is based on technical development as well as on their use by instructors and learners. Neither Dreamweaver nor Flash is particularly suited to design attention management tools, but they enable the creation of simpler tools which support the concept. Links and navigational buttons on a web page can be designed to allow or restrict branching to other areas, unless certain conditions are fulfilled (e.g. completion of certain tasks on the current page). Dreamweaver supports all necessary HTML commands and JavaScript functions (e.g. control flow statements). Flash allows for a more useful implementation in which the learner can be forced back to a certain screen (topic) if he or she has not followed a certain path. Flash can also easily track and correlate performance and time spent online. A diminishing performance, if attributed to fatigue can trigger various system responses: fewer activities, shorter presentations, or a break. Such recommendations can be automated based on continuous logging and analysis of user activities.

Finally, group projects which promote accountability and responsibility are solely the realm of instructional practices. The most technology can accomplish is provide the tools for collaboration: newsgroup, email, calendar, and project management. Online versions of applications similar to (the de facto standard) Microsoft Project are the best venue to proceed. Such online solutions, like iTeamwork.com, can be easily incorporated into a web site designed in Dreamweaver. The embedding can be done at the visual level (frames) or functional (custom API). While such integration is technically feasible in Flash, it is not an elegant approach (due to radically different interface and usability).

Standard 2: Modality Principle

Clark (2003, p.53) describes the *modality principle* which suggests that books and multimedia should use graphics and animations together with text and audio narration. The coordination of audio-visual stimuli overcomes the limited capacity of working memory. These results were re-enforced in a study by Mayer (2001) which compared learning in two different modes: instructional visuals with text and instructional visuals with audio narration. Given the widespread use of multimedia in web-based activities it is almost a given that instructional content should be media rich. However it is imperative that the use of multimedia is done in a way which coordinates multi-sensory inputs. Audio narration, text, and other visuals must support and complement each other.

Well designed instructional media projects will follow the modality principle, which is easily implemented in Adobe (formerly Macromedia) Flash. The ability to synchronize the audio, video, text, and animation layers in Flash allows designers great flexibility in creating content with mutually supportive elements. Furthermore, the ability to bind data from XML repositories allows for separation of the user interface (template) and the content itself. Thus, instructional units with learner (or facilitator) selectable content can accommodate learners at different developmental stages. The support Flash lends to SCORM and Reusable Learning Objects enables designers to easily repurpose and adapt content and be continuously responsive to feedback from learners and instructors.

Standard 3: Contiguity Principle

Clark (2002) describes studies by Sweller, Merrienboer and Paas (1998) which found that graphics and supporting text yield better learning outcomes when combined than when separated. For example, authors often tend to accompany images with textual explanations placed underneath or next to an image. This causes learners to split their attention and process two different objects. The embedding of textual explanation within an image or a video creates a continuity which is easier and more efficiently packaged into working memory. Mayer (2001), the main proponent of the *contiguity principles* found a 68% median gain in learning when using graphics with embedded text.

My own research on networks supports this notion as well. When visually combined, text and graphics are stored in long-term memory already linked. The neural network does not need to create new pathways to build the link between (already) closely related objects.

When designing HTML based instructional material in Dreamweaver for example, web developers usually separate text and graphics as different objects. However while from a programming standpoint they should be separated, there are ways to combine them visually. The support Dreamweaver provides for JavaScript development makes it very easy to add effects like text appearing upon a mouse rollover event. Using the *<box>* element and CSS layers, one can place a text object on top of an image object.

The same functionality can be accomplished in Flash movies. The principles are identical to the one implemented in Dreamweaver, but the implementation is in ActionScript. Furthermore, Flash can as easily embed pictures into text as text into pictures in a manner completely transparent to the user.

Standard 4: Lesson Size

Managing cognitive overload is a topic discussed in most papers on instructional design. It is worth therefore to focus on the main factors which directly affect overload: *lesson size.* It is difficult to decide a priori what an appropriate size is for a lesson in a given course. Online learning, unlike classroom instruction, is not bound by hourly time blocks. Each individual can interact with material within any time frame (within of course reasonable course deadlines). Clark (2003, p. 59) describes that the amount of prior knowledge directly influences the amount of new knowledge that can be assimilated. Differences in the processing capabilities of each learner are also a direct factor in one's learning capacity.

One way to address this issue in modern instructional design is to create sophisticated multimedia units, which automatically adapt to the user performance. For example the system can monitor user feedback, quiz and test results and decide the amount of information displayed on each screen and each lesson. The configuration of each module can be placed in the hands of the instructor. In Dreamweaver, one HTML page could be designed, with several drop-down fields from which the user could select, for example, the number of knowledge blocks to be loaded on a page for each performance level. Again, the implementation of reusable learning objects lends itself natural to this modular approach. It is a bit more difficult to anticipate the size (length) of an HTML page so that it will accommodate a (variable) wide range of page configurations. To some extent one can accomplish this with layers, but it is not elegant from a programming standpoint. Flash is much more friendly in this respect. Basically, there is no interface anyone can dream that cannot be implemented in Flash. Adjusting location and size of a screen as well as all attributes of objects displayed are quite trivially accomplished in ActionScript 2.0. With its ever powerful data binding to MySQL databases (via PHP of course), one can envision designing one interface that can be coupled with an extensive, dynamic database of content blocks (objects), which can accommodate the unique requirements of every single student the system is likely to serve.

Standard 5: Practice Distribution

Closely related to the concept of lesson size is *practice distribution*. This is an additional way to monitor the pace of instruction. The design of an instructional system which supports variable (self-adapting) lesson size impacts primarily the content delivery aspect of a course. The design of an instructional system which supports variable practice distribution impacts the learning process which occurs during the processing phase, after content presentation. Clark (2003) promotes the notion of spaced practice, which spans several segments of instruction delivery. Since students differ in the amount of practice they require an ideal system will sense when such practice is needed as well as its length.

As with most implementation, this is a trivial task in Flash and a bit more cumbersome in Dreamweaver. One way to accomplish this in Dreamweaver is to create short quizzes which will be administered using pop-windows. The windows are easily created with a one-line JavaScript code. The results of the quizzes could either direct the learner to the appropriate (pre-designed) web page, or use dynamic CSS modify the layout of a page and format it to display the desire amount of information. Thus the results of each quiz can dictate whether additional practice is required or the learner can proceed with the current course of events. Furthermore, the results can be stored in cookies so that the learner can log off and return to practice at a later time using the same settings.

Flash can accomplish the same functionality but in a more elegant way. Given the ease with which objects properties like visibility, location, and size can be set the design of dynamic interfaces is trivial. Learning objects can be designed so modularly that they can be mixed and matched at will. Thus quiz questions can be programmed to appear anytime, anywhere on screen. They can lie on top of other objects, blending their visual attributes and become less obstructive to the overall page (screen) design. The timing, frequency and duration are equally easy to accomplish in either Flash or Dreamweaver.

Standard 6: Worked Examples

Atkinson et al (2000) found that learning is positively impacted when students analyze worked example in addition to practice on their own. This finding was particularly true in courses involving problem solving. The best results where achieved when students were given a mixed set of problems: worked examples first, followed by a few unsolved ones, followed by worked examples again. The researchers observed a diminished improvement as learners became more knowledgeable on the topic. In other words, once learning has occurred there is negligible improvement over time.

The same approach used in section 5 above can be implemented here. A good instructional system will detect when a student needs to see more examples, based on performance on regular exercises. Furthermore the exercises can be varied each time, and their level of difficulty increased. When the system detects that a predetermined performance level is reached there is no need for worked examples anymore.

The implementation in Flash or Dreamweaver is identical to the above. It is worth exploring whether the dynamic nature of this application would be better implemented in PHP/MySQL, which both Dreamweaver and Flash support.

Standard 7: Near- and Far-Transfer Tasks

Any learning activity is practically useless if the knowledge gained does not transfer out the classroom (at least indirectly).

While transitioning from one system or environment to another, one is likely to improve performance if in addition to learning how to execute a task one also learns why a given system behaves or reacts the way it does (Clark 2003, p. 151). The working principles of a system or a machine are unlikely to change over a short period of time. Thus it is beneficial to promote understanding of operating principles rather than memorizing a particular implementation sequence. For example, if one understands the steps to follow in order to read schematics of electrical circuits for a simple radio, one could also read schematics for TV sets and DVD players.

Deductive methods consist of instructors making full demonstrations followed by practice sessions. Inductive methods are imposing additional demands (Clark 2003, p. 155). The continuum of transfer promoting strategies is characterized by passive learning (receptive mode) in one extreme and by rich, exploratory activities in the other. The first would be more typical of a behaviorist environment and the latter of a cognitive one. An obvious example of the first (receptive) mode is college lecturing. At the opposite end (exploration) there is the scientific method of hypothesizing, planning experiments, and drawing conclusions.

An efficient way to promote transfer in an in instructional media program is to show and simulate many realistic situations. The technology exists today that allows incorporation of videos and sophisticated animations within a web-based presentation. Dreamweaver supports this approach in several ways. The simplest is including a video object into HTML. In an accounting course for example, it could show a discussion that takes place during an audit of a large corporation. The students could view the video in the context of case studies which have been shown to be very beneficial to learning.

Flash is much more resourceful in the use of (interactive) videos. The same video of a corporate accounting discussion can be enhanced with dynamic interactivity. For example clicking on an area (e.g. one of the accountants) can display information about the person: experience, prior clients, approach to corporate accounting, etc. The video could also include thinking points for students. These points can be dynamically changed to adapt to the level of achievement of the student as it is being tracked by the system. Finally, several segments of video can be recorded and presented, that would respond to learners dynamically changing the numeric data used in the video. Thus learners can experiment with multiple scenarios, all within a Flash application, within a web-browser.

Standard 8: Practice for Supporting Knowledge

Over 20 years ago Merrill (1983) proposed the *Component Display Theory*. With the advent of multimedia and interactive video, Merrill's ideas can not only be validated, but taken to new heights. Every learning activity consists at its core of procedures and principles. Merrill advocated that lessons must also include associated knowledge – facts, concepts, and processes. One main recommendation of this approach is that learners move as quickly as possible from the "remember" level (learning) to the "use" level (application). The main idea is that performing a task induces more learning than discussing about it. Central to this approach is the notion of practicing at performance criteria.

Clark and Mayer (2002) points out that some skills require immediate response to situations, or instinctive reactions. The best way to accomplish this is through intensive drill and practice until the skill and associated facts become hard-wired in long-term memory. Learners can practice in the beginning with learning aids, which can be gradually eliminated. The application of Component Display Theory in this case entails the creation of complex instructional content. Rather than presenting facts, concepts, skills and processes in any particular predetermined order, the presentation can be dynamic, using hyperlinked resources. At the core of a module there can be a particular skill (for example). Key words or images associated with the skill can be hyperlinked to other presentations, videos, simulations, etc. Each one of the supporting modules can in turn become a main topic when accessed, and other supporting topics will appear.

This approach is akin to designing a web page with links to other web pages or with dynamic information changes in different frames on a page. Naturally, this is exactly what Dreamweaver was designed for. As long as the content requires only to user-controlled access and display of objects, Dreamweaver, and supported tools (JavaScript, CSS, PHP) can do a great job. However, the interaction within a (multimedia) object is something outside of its capabilities (and purpose).

Flash movies not only support creative, context sensitive hyper linking but they can be scripted to adapt to the learner's level, interest, and performance. For example live video of a professional business meeting can be overlaid with cues and questions to the learner or with a live text-chat between two or more learners, as if they were participating in the discussion.

Standard 9: Manage and Monitor Meta-cognitive Processes

Vockell (2004) describes a set of pre-requisite skills, which would enable learners to use cognitive skills and strategies effectively. They include ability to monitor their cognitive processes, ability to resist using primitive strategies, possession of an adequate knowledge base, ability to set goals, and ability to transfer thinking strategies to new situations in which they would be appropriate.

Clark (2003, p.184) describes how meta-cognitive skills apply to self-regulated learning. In this context she proposes several activities, which supplement Vockell's: setting specific goals, time management, defining the best tactics to achieve a specific learning goal, monitoring understanding, and making adjustments in tactics based on self-monitoring and evaluation of external feedback.

It is unlikely that educational programs can change the personality of learners. However, just like learners can acquire new knowledge about the world around them they can acquire new knowledge about themselves. Perhaps a chronically procrastinating learner cannot become an efficient time manager. But, a learner aware of the benefits of time management can be taught a few strategies that would improve his or her learning capacity. Instruction delivery should not be limited to teaching a subject matter, but also make the learning experience itself more pleasant, more efficient, and more likely to produce successful individuals. The introspective look into one's capabilities, past successes and failures, and the planning of future goals, are topics which transcend all subjects and greatly influence learner performance, transfer, and personal satisfaction (Brockett and Hiemstra, 1991, p.60).

Instructional media projects can and should easily incorporate tools that foster self-regulated learning and monitor meta-cognitive processes. Such tools can take the form of logs of all interactions between the learner and the system. They can also be more sophisticated and correlate between certain variables, like time spent on classroom discussions and quality (based on grade) of work. More sophisticated tools could compare the learner's performance with that of peers in the class and with others in the program. Finally, these tools can provide recommendations for changes or re-enforcement of current practices the learner follows. Neither Dreamweaver nor Flash is the right tools to accomplish this. While scripts could be written in JavaScript that track usage patterns, this is the realm of Web Analytics Software. Online retailers make extensive use of such tools for customer profiling. Google Analytics is a good, free, tool to get started with in this area. HBX, from WebSideStory is another professional, widely used web analytics tools. Neither of these solutions was designed to track educational performance for self-regulated learning. However, the concept is not foreign to WebCT and Blackboard. Thus instructional developers with good knowledge of WebCT can easily learn and adapt tools like HBX. It is likely that if successful, this approach would lead to the creation of more dedicated tools.

Standard 10: Problem Centered Learning

Savery and Duffy (2001) describe the classical model of *problem based learning (PBL)* first introduced by Barrows and Myers in 1993. The model prescribes that many subjects can benefit from a problem (or case based) approach rather than the traditional lecture and practice. The process involves several distinct chronological steps at the core of which are ideas, facts, learning issues, and an action plan. PBL also encourages group brainstorming and a constructivist exchange of ideas towards reading a solution. Upon concluding the work on problem, the instructor summarizes the topic, presenting knowledge in an abstract way, removing the specifics of the problem analyzed. Those learners are able to move from specific to general cases and eventually apply their newly acquired knowledge to other problems. The process culminates with a phase of self evaluation.

Instructional media projects, especially media rich ones, are perfectly suitable for PBL. In fact the ability to combine multiple sources of information and display it in multiple interactive ways, create unlimited capabilities for presenting problems and cases studies from any domain. A straightforward implementation of a PBK approach using Dreamweaver-centered tools would be the creation of a mini web site. A worthy implementation would consist of A/V clips, simulations, animations, and collaborative tools for exchange of ideas among team members. There isn't a preferred way to implement this in Dreamweaver exclusively or in Flash (for example). PBL offer the opportunity to instructional developers to integrate both tools, Dreamweaver's ability to create complex sites combined with sophisticated learning objects created in Flash are the recommended way to implement a PBL environment.

Summary

Palloff and Pratt (2001, p.152) claim that the delivery method of online instruction is a more dominant factor than content. As evidence, they describe and experiment in which they evaluated a multimedia-rich course (including audio, video, and animations). The course became a failure due to the instructor's lack of experience in online facilitation and community building. Palloff and Pratt emphasize the role of interactivity in designing instruction for the Web.

Instructional media should always be viewed in my opinion as part of a larger educational program. Clark (2003, p. 93-94) cites research that warns against activating too much prior learning, by adding tidbits of information to stimulate interest. Current technology allows for the creation of instructional media, which highly configurable and adaptable to the learner needs and capabilities.

Dreamweaver and Flash are just two tools used to create educational material. They are neither complete nor comprehensive. Instructional developers typically use a variety of tools for the various aspects of educational media productions. Software like Garage Band is very popular for audio editing. Adobe Photoshop and Illustrator are the premier tools for creating graphics. This paper has implicitly and indirectly referred to these tools under the umbrella of Dreamweaver and Flash, themselves packaged as Adobe (formerly Macromedia) Studio.

The creation of instructional media is an evolving art. Tools and techniques available today were not available 10 years ago and they will be superseded 5 years from. While technology advances at an astonishingly rapid pace, our understanding of human cognitive does not. Work done by Merrill, Reigeluth, Gagne, Bandura, and even Pavlov easily endures a few decades. It is therefore imperative that in the quest for the latest technical wizardry one does not lose sight of basic research results, culmination of life time dedication to understanding the processes that govern human learning.

Part IV

Cyber-Ethics

Personal Information and Financial Loan Applications

This essay discusses policies to regulate personal information within the context of financial loan applications. One of the most sensitive issues in the practice of mortgage loan officer is access to an individual's credit report. I would like to discuss this issue in the context of the current practice among some mortgage lenders to outsource loan processing abroad.

The issue

When a customer goes online to one of the popular loan shopping sites, he or she may encounter a statement to the effect that the company is able to save them money by processing the entire application online within minutes because it has a team working around the clock. Often the meaning of this statement is that the company has a team in a different country, in which the combination of cheap labor and time difference allows it to process higher volume, in shorter time and at lower costs.

In many businesses which handle large amounts of paperwork, employees usually leave their current files on their desks when they go home for the day. While the office and the building are secured with combination locks and alarm systems, the overnight cleaning crews have unlimited access to every office and every room.

Similarly, when the employee of the outsourcing firm goes home for the day, most likely his or her files are left on the desk just like it happens in the US. If a cleaning crew can have practically unlimited access to the most sensitive information about one's financial situation, why should we believe that this is any different in other countries?

What if these "other" countries have more lenient privacy protection laws? What is such private information like Social Security Information, bank accounts, assets, employment, address, property tax, financial vulnerabilities, etc. worth for example to an identity thief? What is it worth to a would-be illegal immigrant? What would it be worth to an Al Qaeda operative?

Naturally, for ethical (sic) reasons, I choose not to identify specific mortgage companies nor specific outsourcing countries. However the reasonably talented Internet searcher would have little difficulty in corroborating my above description.

Proposed regulatory action

Bluntly put, I suggest that a law be enacted, *which prohibits the transfer out of the USA of any information submitted by an*

American Citizen or Permanent Resident in conjunction with an
application for a loan.

Such a law would immediately forbid all types of outsourcing within the consumer financial services industry. The legislation is immediately necessary for personal privacy and national security reasons. Furthermore, it is perfectly in line with existing legislation in the EU, namely "Directive 95/46/EC on the protection of individuals with regard to the processing of personal data and the free movement of such data" (Spinello, 2003, p.163). Such legislation prohibits, for example, US based eCommerce sites from collecting user information for marketing purposes, although it allows them to collect such information within the US.

Specifically I propose the following regulatory steps:

1. Personal credit information and financial statements of assets comprise a unique characteristic of an individual. Consequently such uniqueness is akin to a personal profile. It follows that this is therefore the individual's personal property and thus governed by all existing legislation regarding personal property.

2. The misuse, misleading use, abuse, intentional or non intentional use, or other handling of an individual's personal credit and financial information, without the expressed written consent of the individual is a crime equal in severity

with rape, harassment, and personal assault. The most severe
existing punishment for the above crimes should be adapted
to the proposed legislation.

3. The term "secured transaction" in the context of an Internet-
    based financial inquiry or loan application should extend to
    any physical location the collected application may end.
    Consequently, all financial service providers should
    implement physical security measures to protect all
    information collected from its customers within 90 days of
    the enactment of the proposed legislation.

4. All new and existing employees within the financial services
    sector must receive appropriate training regarding cyber and
    physical security of Internet-collected information, within 60
    days of the enactment of the proposed legislation.

5. A regulatory commission should be established, under the
    jurisdiction of the FTC. The proposed commission will
    monitor, audit and enforce compliance with security
    measures called by this proposal.

6. Apart from federal legislation, it is recommended that the US
    government start collaboration talks with the EU aimed at
    ultimately creating a global cyber-space in which private

individual information enjoys uniform protection under all national legislations of Internet-user states.

Some concrete, although insufficient steps in this direction have already been taken by several countries. For example, the Canadian Civil Liberties Association (CCLA, 2004) has influenced the Canadian government to adopt the European concept that "privacy is central to human dignity and liberty." (CCLA, 2004). This is an encouraging step on the international stage further validates my recommendation.

In spite of Financial Modernization Act of 1999 (FTC, 2004) also known as the "Gramm-Leach-Bliley Act" or GLB Act, it appears current provisions in the law are insufficient for the protection of personal financial information held by financial institutions. This further strengthens my argument that clear, tough legislation is needed.

In 2000 the FTC submitted a report to Congress (FTC, 2000) in which an encouraging picture was portrayed of 47% of US Internet companies surveyed implemented some form of privacy protection unit. However, "Even if the Commission majority, who endorse the Report, determined that our experience was insufficient to assess offline privacy concerns, a better course would have been to invite further Congressional inquiry." (FTC, 2000, p. 106).

Final word

While proponents of tougher privacy protection legislation argue its various incarnations, there are others who oppose leaving open doors to governmental legal intrusions into ones' private affairs. McCullagh (2004) states that 2,200,000 wiretaps were court-approved in 2002. McCullagh, while an independent journalist, provides the basis for an ongoing debate regarding the Patriot Act. It appears that the tradeoff between privacy, security and ethics is still far from a consensus point.

Ethical Challenges in Global Communities of Distance Educators

This essay reflects on the ethical challenges that will be encountered by the formation of a global community of distance educators. I would like to discuss the ethical challenges within the context of two major aspects of the teaching profession: instructional design and professional development.

Instructional design

The creation of lesson plans, learning units, and course syllabi is daunting. The ability to be creative on demand, to be clear and explicit, comprehensive yet focused on learning objectives is an art. Mastery of this art often marks the distinction between a good teacher and an outstanding educator. The availability of massive amounts of electronic documents teachers can find on the Internet can often alleviate the difficulty in creating quality educational material.

The ethical dilemma is what can we copy freely and what should we ask permission for? Is education such a noble goal that an educator pressed to create a new unit overnight can just simply copy and paste one from wherever a Google ™ search happens to land? After all, aren't educators underpaid, overworked and underappreciated? After all, isn't all educational material posted on the Internet public domain de facto?

I found it amusing that the Institute for Global Ethics website returned "Sorry. No document matches your search." in response to a search on *plagiarism*. It is anecdotal, but nevertheless an indicator of how subjective the subject of ethics can be.

On the Open University of the UK one can find useful information that can be helpful in creating a new class. For example course a 12-page guide to course H850, Postgraduate Certificate in Teaching and Learning in Higher Education. It can provide valuable information in terms of learning outcomes, lesson planning and course design. The dilemma still exists about "justified" plagiarism.

I believe a more definitive answer to this dilemma is provided by the Massachusetts Institute of Technology's Open Courseware initiative. MIT has decided to make available online free of charge entire body of educational material created by its faculty. MIT invites everyone to use its materials even to the extent of creating entire curricula. This is MIT's way of giving back to the educational community some of the fruits of its vast research and educational endeavors.

This pretty much answers the dilemma presented above: unless you are given explicit permission to use (educational) materials, the ethical and moral approach would simply be to look, get inspiration, and create your own.

Professional development

In addition to providing the opportunity to deliver education over the Internet, the distance learning paradigm can be applied to the concept of virtual corporation.

There is nothing to prevent online educators who already collaborate (or at list discuss) online to form their own online schools. On the face of things there is no problem here, after all mortgage loan officers do it all the time – and they take their customers with them, in effect stealing a portion of the customer base of their former employer.

Since distance education providers are largely for profit corporations, losing students can mean losing significant income. However, there is an opportunity for an entrepreneurial, underpaid, under-appreciated and "under-titled" online instructor to create a new virtual school. In that new school, one can assume titles like Dept. Chair, Dean or even President, with the same rights as one would start any new small business.

The myriad of unaccredited online education providers, or semi-accredited "universities" allows one to quickly advance professionally bypassing the traditional norms established by 2000 years of (European) educational institutions.

No doubt, one can do the same in the non-Internet world, but logistically it is so much easier to create a web site than rent a building. Ad hoc instructional principles, departments, and corporate hierarchy can be established without particular attention to regulation. After all education can be a business providing products and services just like any other business.

If I have a few failing students who are willing to pay to graduate, I could team up with colleagues I find on the Internet and start a new business which is instantly funded by its customers (i.e. students) whom I would transfer from my previous employer. Case in point, ABET Open University, which offers an MBA online, in 6 months, for $384, or $584 if you wish to study in French.

To the extent that accreditation can be addressed satisfactorily per students' needs this is a legitimate endeavor whose unethicality would be hard to prove in a court of law. To this effect the International Council for Open and Distance Education, advertises as its purpose to "promote public confidence that the quality of standards and provision of services to students in Open and Distance Learning are being safeguarded."

Ethical Principles and Distance Learning

This essay discusses three topics regarding ethical principles and distance learning. When will global communities of distance educators require a set of universally agreed upon ethical principles? Because of the distance involved in physical proximity among online learners, is there a difference (from face-to-face situations) in how ethical sensitivities to a culturally diverse learner base must be approached? Is there a growing consensus on the nature of these principles?

Communities of Distance Educators and Ethical Principles

Since time immemorial neighboring societies tried to forge commercial and military alliances. These alliances were designed to help grow the economic and military strength and stability of their members. Gradually de facto standards or approximate standards have emerged in such areas like measurement units, weights, monetary exchange and damage assessment.

The spread of military conquest and the establishment of great empires, be them physical like Rome or cultural like present day US have always contributed and are continuously contributing to the adoption of universally agreed methods, practices, and principles.

When agreement is not unanimous, methods for conversion from one set of standards to another are employed.

In this respect the global community of distance educator is just one link in the multidimensional array if chains which comprises our (global) society. Also in this respect, the Internet is just one (the latest) conduits for communicating, disseminating and exchanging views about emerging practices and principles in education as in many other fields.

I do not believe there will be a noticeable point in time at which distance educators will adopt a set of universally agreed upon ethical principles. Such principles will be gradually adhered to (like anti-plagiarism) while others will coexist in multiple forms across the Internet (like the equivalence between prior-non academic knowledge and academic requirements). Colero (2002) writes that *"In a sense, the principles are outcomes of the mother of all principles - unconditional love and compassion - which appears in virtually all faiths, and is expressed here as 'concern for the well-being of others'. (This principle is at the heart of the stakeholder model of ethics, i.e. what is my impact on others?)"*

Just like military force and trade are the major catalysts of global affairs so they will influence distance education. Distance educators share the Internet with online shops, stock brokers, military analysts, entertainers, and news agencies. Therefore it is only natural that there is cross-industry transfer of knowledge practices and or course ethical principles.

Copying a lesson plan is no different than copying a logo. Evaluating a history assignment is no different than evaluating a company stock. Managing online discussion in a Math class is no different than managing an online discussion on product specifications among engineers.

The emergence of such cross-industry terminology like edutainment and advergaming is an indication of the communication that exists among Internet-based enterprises. I believe that the constant exposure to each other's practices will mutually influence businesses and educational providers to gradually gravitate towards de facto agreed upon ethical practices. In turn they will be followed by more formal agreements as is the case for example with the ongoing debate on regulations for privacy protection between the US and the European Union.

Ethical Sensitivities to a Culturally Diverse Learner Base

Education is a two-way process in many respects. Culturally diverse learning communities of students and educators face the challenge of mutual recognition and adaptation to their respective differences.

Providers of education might be interested in designing lesson plans that take into account gender sensitivities in different cultures. On the other hand learners must comply with sensitivities important to the educator if one is to attend an online class in a different country or society. In this context Jackson and Chernish

(2004) note that *"Ethnic barriers may be addressed by tailoring distance programs, or by creating peer groups with similar learning backgrounds and interests. Illustrations in distance learning delivery can include culturally appropriate personal names and culturally accepted phrases. This illustration does not confuse any theoretical offerings. Rather, it embraces the background of the student and serves as an engaging point to keep their interest."*

If an online school wishes students to enroll in its classes it must provide educational products that are sought by its students. Conversely, if students wish to obtain a degree from a given school they must comply with the requirements of that school. In this respect there is no difference between online and face to face instruction. However, there is a difference in which distance education can accommodate for differences in ways traditional education cannot.

For example, the requirement by a society to separate between men and women in a classroom can be easily accommodated online. Additional physical structures are neither required, nor additional educators nor learning materials. When all resources are virtual there is an unlimited supply. Furthermore, cross-gender dialogs which could not exist in a physical classroom can occur regularly online.

Distance education provides solutions to two other culture-based needs of learners: language and national/religious holidays. An online instructor in Pakistan (for example) can teach in Pashto to Pakistani learners enrolled at an online school in Argentina. The

Pakistani instructor does not have to relocate and therefore can be easily hired to match the particular needs of a Pakistani class. Furthermore, there would be no need to explain why some assignments could not be submitted on time by students observing a certain holiday. The Executive MBA program at the University of Dallas is actually implementing the dispersed faculty and students approach: *"International faculty and geographically dispersed students create a cross-cultural learning experience."*

In general the accessibility to a variety of educators can accommodate the most specific of students request. Therefore the driving force behind cultural accommodation is business. If there are students willing to purchase a certain online educational product, then the Internet can enable the congruence of resources required to deliver that product.

Consensus on the Nature of Principles

I do not think one can formulate a conclusive opinion on the status of consensus among distance educators and within the educational community.

While the Internet provides unprecedented conduits for wide adoption of standards it also provides unprecedented opportunity for individualism. One can see for example some uniformity in the way instruction is delivered - HTML pages, email, newsgroups, and alike.

On the other hand one can also see divergence of opinions on content, emphasis, and institutional credibility.

Roughly 400 years of American higher education practices are hard to change by traditional colleges. Even more so can be said about the much older European universities. On the other hand online universities do not have to be like other (existing) universities. In fact they highlight the non-conformist nature of their approach to learning and instruction delivery. For example in a traditional university Chemistry class students would be expected to attend a lab. However, distance learning compels schools to come up with innovative alternatives – kitchen Chemistry:"*Because they use materials readily available at grocery and hardware stores, and involve techniques no more dangerous than boiling water, the experiments don't require specialized laboratory facilities or close supervision by a trained laboratory instructor. Because they involve making measurements on real chemicals found in the home, they bring the sights, sounds and conditions of experimental science to the place where students do most of their real life chemistry, their kitchens.*" (Reeves and Kimbrough).

I will use a fictitious but plausible example to illustrate my point. If two countries are signatories to a treaty that mutually recognizes accredited college degrees online institutions enjoy the same benefit.

Therefore I find a country with loose accreditation requirements I can easily establish a school in that country and legitimately offer recognized, accredited degrees in the US. As long as my students meet the requirements of the country in which is base my Web home page and my mail address is recognized by the hoist country as the address of my university, and as long the host country is signatory to a treaty with the US, American institutions will recognize that degree as legitimate.

The same "scheme" can be employed in a much more positive, constructive way. For example, traditional old school can partner across the Internet with emerging schools and provide joint degrees, instantly accredited in two countries. Carliner (2001) describes the administration of such partnership as efficient in addressing such common issues like scheduling conflicts, class cancellations, limited curriculum, instructor availability, and other.

This was just one dimension of what is possible and is currently happening in the world of distance education. While the emergence of a universal set of principle is still elusive, let alone consensus on one, it is safe to assume that creativity is on the rise in all aspects of online education. From software to accreditation, from recognizing prior experience to culturally individualized programs, distance education providers are redefining education delivery itself. On this I am sure there is widespread consensus.

Ethical Issues in Distance Education

Distance education presents many challenges. For most people it evokes connotations of learners and instructors exchanging messages online. As an insider, at times learner, at times facilitator, at times software developer, and at times marketing executive, I had the opportunity to become intimately acquainted with the complexities of distance education. At the core of this learning environment there is an ongoing debate focused on the legitimacy and quality of the Internet-based, asynchronous learning model. In part, this debate originates in the ethical and moral challenges this model presents.

Ethical Issues

Gert writes in (Spinello & Tavani 2004) that "We believe that an explicit, clear, and comprehensive account of morality would help to make clear the uncontroversial nature of many moral decisions." Given the lack of universal moral and ethical guidance on the Internet, there are several ethical issues in which I am foremost interested, in the context of distance education

Student authentication and identification – how can the instructor verify that the person who claims to have written an assignment and even participated in class is really the one he or she claims to be? Furthermore, who bears the responsibility for such verification? Should students and educational institutions be required to install visual or perhaps biometric identification mechanisms as a requirement for regional accreditation?

Right to privacy (or the right to remain silent) – One could argue that in traditional classroom environments it is possible for students to remain silent for long periods of time (days or weeks). Their choice of "private" communication via written assignments and their lack of classroom participation do not necessarily impact their score if their written performance is outstanding. Internet based distance education forces participation upon these students. Should the instructor penalize a "silent" student or is a "silent" student not suitable for such a learning environment? Is there a basis for a debate on discriminatory implications?

Technological gap – Students as well as instructors view technology is either a friend or a phobia. Distance learning environments require that Humanities students be as proficient in certain technical areas as Science students. Even among the so called non-technically inclined persons, there are wide differences in their ability to exploit electronic databases, search engines and other useful Internet-based tools. To the extent that good command of Internet-based technologies is an asset in an Internet-based learning environment should there be an equalizing or at least compensating educational or evaluative factor?

Authenticity of information – Traditional textbooks undergo a tedious process of review and edit prior to their distribution to retail stores.

This process can often take many months. The Internet has the capability to spread information at the speed of light, literally. There is no mechanism to validate information published on blogs, chat rooms and on personal web sites. Consequently, the same instrument, popularity, which is the ultimately measure of success of a textbook, becomes a potentially dangerously misleading element for Internet-based information dissemination.

Online Student Identification

One of the major ethical problems with distance education is student identification. An online educational environment relying on e-mail as its primary means of communication is incapable of authenticating the student submitting online assignments.

Authentication could be at least enhanced if not guaranteed by the use of personal intrusive identifiers during each online session. Such identifiers include combinations of Social Security Number and unique computer processor ID (Spinello, 2003, p. 166). Other means would be writing style matching against stored essays and other written work collected when the student first applied to the school. Additional stronger means could include a variety of biometric technologies like finger printing digitally transmitted via the Internet.

The notion of academic freedom has certain connotation within the context of student-teacher and student-school interaction. It implies a certain degree of trust that those affiliated with an educational institution have the "right" moral convictions and would not abuse their freedom. Spinello proposes (p. 170) "the primacy of ethical self-regulation facilitated by code" as a way to balance institutional intrusion (e.g. the government) with that of market needs. Since for all intents and purposes the exchange of ideas among students and instructors is akin to commercial exchange of goods and services, Spinello's suggestion seems adaptable to educational institutions as well.

It is obvious that regulating Internet activities infringe on one's personal rights. What remains to be debated is merely the extent of the infringement. Do doctoral students n such writing intensive programs like Education have the right to expect a little credit for decency and morality not to cheat on their assignments? Is submission of homework late at 3 am not reliable testimony of one's commitment to academic honesty?

The same Internet used for distance education is being used for eBusiness. Consequently the atmosphere of mistrust created by such issues like identity theft and credit card fraud is bound to relate negative connotations to all Internet activities, including distance learning. Within such a climate it is debatable whether some percentage of the online student and faculty population can maintain the traditional academic freedoms of expression. Is academic honesty compromised because some do not really share what they think for fear that their words would appear on some unsympathetic Website within a few hours?

Gearhart (2001) cites a US Department of Justice report finding that "When we interact with others face-to-face we see the results immediately of inappropriate and unethical behaviors. When we use information technology in a way that does harm to others, the act feels less personal because we can't see or hear the other person in the exchange." If we translate this finding into a distance learning environment, the implication would be that a student not having to see the instructor face to face has less moral constraints against cheating. This finding is disturbingly conflicting with the expectation of honesty suggested above. The US DoJ refers to the notion of "psychological distance" (Gearhart, 2001) as being conducive to dishonest behavior. The implication to online education is that the more freedom and privacy we afford distant students, the more likely we are to create an environment predisposed to dishonesty.

Bowden and Akdeniz (1999) quote a British government report recommendation that "would also allow the Government to ban oral discussions and dissemination of abstract mathematical research, without further primary legislation." While at prima facie this recommendation represents a further erosion of academic freedom, appearances can be deceiving. The apparent conflict between regulatory needs and the right to privacy can be traced back several hundred years.

One could claim that the invention of the printing press, for example, created a medium for quick duplication and dissemination of information, analogous to the Internet. Once information (or disinformation) was printed and the text disseminated, it became public domain and thus subject to public scrutiny and debate. Out of context and incomplete information could have been quickly made available to the masses in the form of printed newsletters or pamphlets and thus undermining – at least temporarily – the individual's expectation (if not right) to privacy. Schulman (2004) found that apart from the ethical debate, the Internet is transforming social and academic discourse and interaction. She quotes a research by Millora stating that "young people truly believe that everyone in the world is part of their community. Computers, the Web—that's their mechanism for building community."

Similar issues can be translated to other breakthrough mass communication technologies like telephony and telegraphy. The natural course of social evolution seems to have coped successfully with integrating any such new technologies. I am therefore confident the current debates will eventually become the catalysts for moral, ethical and normative transformation of society. As Internet related technologies inundate every single aspect of our private and public lives, I believe they will in time become so ubiquitous that they will be relegated to non-issue status.

The Need for Personalization of Student Performance Assessment

Current diversification of learning media (classroom, Web, video, email, etc.) calls for a reform in student performance assessment. As the prospect for personalized academic programs becomes more realistic, there is an imperative to institute personalized assessment as well. Trust, student identification, and plagiarism are but few of the issues that have transgressed time and technologies to "haunt" distance education institutions to this very day. Personalization can and should be adequately implemented while addressing ethical concerns of students, instructors, their peers and their (educational) institutions. Online instructors have a responsibility for creating an environment that encourages academic honesty. Their primary tools are psychological and intended to stimulate and motivate students to the point where they would consider it totally unbecoming to impersonate or plagiarize. It is harder to motivate students you don't see, but one-on-one communication can go a long way. Although such communication is available to face-to-face instructors, it is often neglected due to the in-class group meetings. The online environment creates the opportunity to better exploit the power of personal communication and assessment.

Introduction

Between 1994 and 1999 the percentage of US public schools connected to the Internet has increased from 35% to 95% (National Center of Educational Statistics, 2000). One could only extrapolate from that data that in 2005 all US public schools are connected to the Internet.

A new generation of students is growing without being able to imagine a world without the Internet. Students learn more when they are creating their own learning opportunities (Bradford, 2005). This realization will contribute to Internet-based learning being integrated into "traditional", face-to face instruction. This integration will require focused attention on issues like user authentication, significant classroom participation, and electronic plagiarism. The integration process will be driven by students rather than by schools (American Institutes for Research, 2002).

Some students prefer to be silent in public but are prolific writers. Others do not write well, but can skillfully make a thorough verbal argument. Research has shown that technology will enable learners to find their preferred venue for personal expression thus enabling students who would normally be quiet and/or shy in a physical classroom to strive in an online environment (Dolog and Sintek, 2004).

Thus, a major ethical dilemma will rise with the need to evaluate student performance in a highly individualized environment. Ultimately education, pedagogy, and instructional design will evolve to a point at which individualized programs will allow direct and personalized interaction and performance assessment between each student and the instructor (Petula, 2004).

Ethical Aspects of E-learning and Personalization

One of the characteristics of Internet-based learning is the absence of a physical classroom and hence the absence of face-to-face social interaction with peers and the instructor. Some people work and perform differently in a group than alone.

Danchak (2005) explains how environments designed for diverse learning styles can also help expand learning repertoires. In this context, there are three important ethical aspects to consider:

e. A defining attribute of ethical conduct is fairness. The potential for unfairness in individual evaluation due to the uniqueness of each student-instructor interaction in the absence of the equalizing effect of the (physical) group.

f. The potential for student fraud (e.g. plagiarism, impersonation) due to the absence of authentication mechanisms, especially in the context of major tests and theses.

g. The relationship between an academic program and the transfer of learning outcomes into the workplace is vaguely established. We often witness the inadequacy of a program in preparing students for a professional career. It is unethical for a school to teach skills (for example) that are outdated or inapplicable just because it uses generic evaluation methods that do not account for the variety of applications its students will face in the workplace. Weller (2004) supports this idea by stating that "By using a learning-object approach, it is feasible to create courses on the fly that will be well suited to the individual learner....They will be better suited to learning within the workplace and are well suited to a just-in-time approach." Weller in turn brings additional supportive citations for need to individualize the learning experience. Weller quotes Lave and Wagner stating that "while training company providers are also engaged in this reuse activity, they are aiming at what they perceive to be a much bigger market: content aggregation on the fly by individual learners or training providers." Finally, the ADL Initiative of the US Army (SCORM) states that its purpose "is to ensure access to high-quality education and training materials that can be tailored to individual learner (ADL Initiative).

A more detailed examination of each one of these aspects is now in order. Traditional face-to-face classroom interaction, combined with in-person meetings in the instructor's office, greatly reduce the need for additional communication with students. In a distance learning environment the only way to communicate is electronic, mostly via email. The lack of a multi-sensory interaction leads to a one-dimensional expression of a student's knowledge and talents – writing ability.

Students who can express themselves very well orally but are less talented writers will be penalized by the absence of their strongest compensating factor. In a traditional classroom the student might get credit for active participation, intelligent comments and catalyzing effect on the group. Conversely, in a distance learning class, the instructor will not be even aware that the student possesses any verbal skills let alone that they might be superior to the writing ones.

A second very important ethical aspect of Internet based learning is embodied in the widespread concern about user authentication and identity-theft in all Internet-based activities. While there are many technologies available for the facilitation of distance education, now the overwhelming majority of programs rely on email and news groups, i.e. communication in writing. When most interaction between students and teachers is in the form of written communication there is simply no way the instructor can ensure that authenticity of the writer behind emails, papers and tests. Instructors are forced to evaluate the work submitted to them with complete disregard for the person behind. Such defacing of personality can have a negative effect on the studious, ethical student and a great positive effect on the fraud-inclined student.

There are schools that require more rigorous student authentication. Northcentral University, for example requires that graduation exams are taken in person or via video conferencing. However, the fact that few online schools have such requirements might have negative implications on the image online schools would like to project. One could interpret this as a sign that distance-learning institutions are simply not concerned with student authentication issues. This in turn can have a damaging effect on the reputation of such institutions and on the credibility of their academic evaluation and degrees conferred. Therefore, it would benefit these institutions to increase their awareness of such weaknesses and at least announce a remedial policy.

Good instructional design and a secure, educationally compelling learning platform are the two main tools distance-learning institutions can employ to mitigate the problems described earlier. The third troubling aspect of Internet learning is related to the mapping of classroom knowledge to real world needs. Before expanding on this idea, some clarifications are in order.

Schweber (2005) cites a survey by the Sloan Foundation which estimates that in the US 2,634,189 students were enrolled in at least one online class in Fall 2004. Most students enrolled in distance education do so in order to acquire a degree, which will advance their career. Therefore it is fair to assume that unlike liberal arts colleges for example, distance learning colleges have embarked on a mission to provide useful skills and knowledge to its students. This assumption is augmented by the corporate marketing efforts made by some of the bellwethers of the distance education industry like University of Phoenix and Capella University, whose aggressive Internet banner ad campaign is impossible to ignore.

The Internet is omnipresent in business, entertainment, commerce, and education. The exposure of online schools to requirements by industry and society in respect to knowledge and skills students should acquire in college is direct and transparent. When students "attend" classes from their office desks, their homes, or even Internet-cafes, online schools become instantly plugged into each student's lifestyle and personal environment. Failure of online schools to adapt evaluation of acquired knowledge and skills to individuals' needs and requirements amounts to providing misleading testimony of mastery of knowledge and skills. While the intent would be the decisive factor in assessing culpability, the mere adoption of a blanket approach to testing and certification would be an indication of an outdated educational program at best and of an unethical one at worst.

Current Practices in Student Performance Assessment

The common practice for evaluating student performance in Internet-based classes is the assessment of regular submissions of written work. Some universities, like the University of Phoenix require that students log on and "post comments at least four out of seven days each week" Daily written emails combined with larger weekly written assignments are largely the only tools online instructors are currently using to evaluate students' work. Some schools, like Northcentral University require that final thesis defense be conducted via videoconference precisely to eliminate the potential for impersonation. However, additional assistance and coaching which might take place at the student's location cannot be detected from the instructor site.

Some instructors make an effort to interact with students often and give them the opportunity to comment or resubmit their work. The idea is that frequent interaction will acquaint the instructor with a particular student's style of expression and thus increase the ability of detecting identity fraud.

Current Technologies for Personalizing Online Student Teacher Interaction

Current Internet technologies enable communication via text, voice, video, and any combination of the three. The availability of low cost, high quality voice over IP telephony offered by companies like Skype™, combined with high speed Internet available on mobile phones, mean that anyone can communicate with anyone else without concern for high costs of long-distance calls.

Services like eFax™ and JFax™ enable one to submit recorded voice messages as attachments to emails. The same can be done with video. Thus a written assignment can be easily augmented with multimedia types of communication that will add a human face to an email or a paper. Naturally the same technology can be employed by instructors who could send recorded voice or video messages to students in addition to comments on a paper, for example.

With the low cost and high availability of high speed Internet virtually on any communication device, the ability of live video conference between students and instructor is a feasible reality. Specifically in such classes that teach skills, the ability to guide the students in a multi-sensory environment can greatly enhance the acquaintance of the instructor with the student abilities, objectives, attitude, and personality in general.

Other technologies like electronic white boards and application sharing, can allow students to see a live demonstration of using a particular software tool or developing a mathematical formula directly on their screen. That demonstration can be captured and save on the student computer or on a website for repeated viewing.

The availability of such tools can enable instructors to employ such proven techniques like instant quizzes and teach-back. Thus, the instructor can immediately assess a student's strengths and weaknesses and decide on remedial action or increased level of difficulty.

The Discord between Individualization, Privacy and Assessment Methods

When a person applies for a credit card or a mortgage loan, several individual parameters are taken into consideration by the lender: age, income, credit score, length of employment past late payments, debt level, and debt to income ratio, the purpose and size of the loan, the assets available as collaterals, and several other factors. Thus, the lender can create a unique profile and tailor a product for that specific individual. Furthermore, the applicant has the option of matching his or her unique circumstance, needs, and goals with similar products offered by other lenders.

The financial services industry as well as its customers are simultaneously extremely concern with privacy, user authentication, security as it is with personalized service. This is an example of convergence of needs and objectives, which lead to workable, efficient solutions.

In contrast, distance learning combines disregard for personal privacy, information security and user authentication with a one-product-fits-all philosophy. The generic evaluation of specific, partial sets of a student's demonstrated abilities can potentially lead to two unwarranted situations:

(a)   over-valuation based on a "lucky strike" – good performance on a written assignment; or

---

(b)   under-valuation based on partial information about the
         students' overall ability

To the extent that colleges pretend to prepare students for a
professional career, the uni-dimensional aspect of current assessment
methods is presenting students with a distorted picture of the real
world at best. At worst, it inhibits their other skills and potentially
handicaps their future development.

The Case for Personalization

The expectation that college education culminates with a set
of skills transferable to the real world and the workplace has been
discussed earlier. Let us examine a few of the requirements of the real
world and workplace and establish how personalized assessment can
fulfill them.

Already in 1991 Lehman and Granger reported that "Empire
State College ... specifically addresses the evaluation issues raised by
an individualized educational program for adults. Empire State's
program provides for an individually designed degree plan and
learning contracts ... In a fundamental sense, an individualized
educational program requires an individualized assessment strategy
(Hodgkinson 1975). Until recently however, individualized
assessment seemed prohibitively difficult and expensive for most
colleges." "Recently" was 15 years ago for Lehman and Granger.

Behaviorist learning approaches advocate the principle of "practice at performance criteria". These criteria are the result of reconciling two sets of requirements. The first is that presented by a student's current or potential future career. The second is the expression of a student's personal goals. In the absence of concrete personal objectives or outside dictated ones it would be impossible to assess whether a student has successfully completed a task or passed a course.

The following specific, hypothetical but plausible examples will help illustrate this point. An individual takes an online class in College Algebra 1. One of the topics in this class is solving a system of linear equations. Let us examine the circumstances of three students enrolled in this class.

Bob takes this class because it is a required class in Bachelor degree in Chemistry. Bob must demonstrate the ability to solve a system of linear equations. Although a grade of C is enough to fulfill the program requirements Bob aspires to get an A in the class. Jane takes the class because the employer pays tuition and there will be a salary increase. Jane must pass the class with a minimum grade of D, which could happen even if she fails one exam. Pat plans to become a high-school Math teacher. Pat must demonstrate the ability to solve systems of linear equations as well as to teach the skill. Pat must pass the class with a minimum grade of B. It is worth noting that current curricula differentiate between learning content and learning content delivery (teaching). Distance (and personalized) education offers the opportunity to embed teaching skills in a content-oriented class, thus eliminating the need to take a different, generic teaching class, or perhaps augment the generic one. It is obvious that Bob and Jane do not have to demonstrate teaching abilities; Pat does not necessarily need an A; Bob will do anything to get the highest grade possible; Jane will do the minimum to pass and could not care less about the second after the class is over.

This scenario can be easily applied to many other disciplines. As such, it typifies the need for individualized performance assessment. Internet based learning offers many opportunities and means for such assessment. Specifically, the asynchronous learning model allows students to prepare and submit their assignments independent of other students. This has tremendous advantages in the hypothetical scenario described above.

For example Bob can request additional sets of problem or higher level of difficulty in order to demonstrated a higher mathematical aptitude worthy of an A grade. Bob, a Chemistry student must demonstrate analytical skills in addition to mechanical ones. Jane will choose to be tested on easiest sections and not "waste" time on material she never indents to remember anyway. Pat will be required to submit a video recording of teaching a module in order to demonstrate teaching abilities. Pat may also be required to take an additional unit in instructional design. The possibility of creating rich learning material with hyperlinks to optional units and with customized success criteria can easily enables Bob, Jane, and Pat to fulfill their individual goals, independent of each other and within the same class.

Rossman wrote in 2002 in support of individualized assessment that "In time our mass-produced standard subject-matter tests would be replaced with individualized testing that adequately takes account of unique learning style, talents, opportunities, needs, handicaps, limitations diagnosis. At each periodic examination the questions and procedures should take account of the learning history of the individual, should propose programs for deficiencies and more."

The modularity of Internet-based instruction can lead to a true assessment of student performance in comparison with stated objectives and success criteria. As long as these criteria are clearly stated and an agreed upon interpretation of evaluation results is established the road is open for individualized assessment. Swan (2001) in a research on interactions and online learning cites Kashy's finding that "ongoing assessment of student performance linked to immediate feedback and individualized instruction supports learning."

Some might argue that an individualized approach might be confusing and a grade of B, for example might reflect different things for different people. Thus, the argument would go, it would be very hard to assess in a credible way the true value of a student course evaluation or even the evaluation of an entire academic degree.

Moore (2004) cites strong evidence for a preference for adaptive, personalized learning and assessment experience in computer based training and distance learning environments. "In the University at Albany's computer and media education courses, students participate in and learn to create lesson plans incorporating rubrics—not only do rubrics help assess student performance, by helping students focus on what matters in the course, they help refine the course and reduce questions... Michigan State University uses LON-CAPA, open-source freeware for assessment and content management, to obtain immediate, detailed feedback about online homework, which can be used to quickly adjust lectures, recitation sessions, and individual help to address learner needs."

My position is that we apply the same approach to each individual course and each individual students, just like we individualize loan application, workplace performance, home decoration, or external appearance to name a few. Personalization is easy and computers and the Internet make it even easier. The communication is individual, the goals and objectives are individual and the degree is conferred by the institution to the individual. The only missing piece in this "puzzle" is individual performance assessment. Graves (2004) in his recommendation for academic redesign states that "The instructor, working with any assistants who might be involved in the instructional process, can design strategies for individualized student interventions by using [...] continuous assessment strategies"

Finally, some students will likely develop new skills throughout their program of study. Therefore, it is only natural to expect that they should be allowed to express themselves through their newly acquired skills.

The Pitfalls of Personalization

The personalization of student teacher interaction in general of performance assessment in particular poses some problems for instructors, students, and institutions alike. Undoubtedly the need to maintain and monitor a different set of requirements for each student may be a daunting task for some teachers and perhaps even unmanageable for others. Widespread adoption of such a concept might steer away many would-be good teachers, especially those who perceive themselves as overworked and/or underpaid.

While macro level differences among schools are accepted by society (as are differences among business service providers and among employers), micro level differences among evaluation methods in an educational program or among students in the same class might be harder to accept. Society as a whole would have to undertake a reform in its thinking about performance assessment. Companies would have to continuously synchronize their requirements with education providers. Employees would have to continuously reassess their career goals in light of the myriad of new venues available.

Universities might be required to provide degrees and programs a-la-carte with operational and logistical costs outweighing

the academic benefits, noble as they may be. Not all students are
capable of outlining and defining clear educational objectives. The
misidentification of such objectives or shifting career goals may lead
to a program of study that to focused. A highly customized degree or
course may hinder a student's ability to transfer knowledge into a
different environment, profession or employer. Thus students might
be compelled to repeat certain classes or take more classes than
originally planned thus lengthening the duration of their studies and
increase cost.

Conclusion - Personalization Will Overcome Ethical Concerns

The counter-arguments to personalized assessment are strong
if one considers them on the context of present social norms, present
business practices and established educational traditions. However,
any reform, especially a conceptual one must rely on vision,
extrapolation into near and distant future trends and understanding of
driving forces change. Let us examine how personalized assessment
is a necessity called for by industry needs, alignment with personal
life, and how it can be easily implemented with current and emerging
technology.

Moore and Lorenzo (2002) cite Joeann Humbert, Director of
Online Learning at Rochester Institute of Technology: "Online
learners, like customers, are satisfied when they receive responsive,

timely, and personalized services and support." What does it mean to have a Bachelors degree in Chemistry? Assuming one can answer this question, the subsequent question would be what does it mean to graduate with a 3.5 GPA as opposed to a 3.1? Does it make one more employable? Does it make one more knowledgeable? A better fit for a company? Should these questions even be asked or should they be left to employers to uncover during the hiring interview or on-the-job assessment period?

The personalization of performance assessment advocated in this paper eliminate these dilemmas. It allows students and instructors to establish precise educational objectives at the onset of one's academic studies. Then, over the course of study every individual skill can be measured against the pre-established, specific learning outcomes. Such learning outcomes can be defined by the learner, by current or potential employers, by an academic advisor, or by any combination of the three.

The ED Anywhere website describes an innovative high school diploma distance learning program, STARS, in which "curriculum and instructional staff will be able to measure the programs performance at the student level, through STARS ability to provide individualized testing, assessment, and remedial instruction. It will enable teachers to intercede immediately in a student's educational program when conditions indicate that help is needed."

Graves (2004) observes that "The instructional process can be individualized, in conjunction with continuous assessment strategies and individualized intervention strategies, to accommodate the disparate learning styles and learning accomplishments of different students as they navigate the course's learning objectives."

The EEC Team's challenge response in the Sloan-C Online Research Workshop, Spring 2004 outlined several principles for blended, asynchronous learning environments. Particularly relevant to this paper are their recommendations regarding individualization and assessment (EEC Team, 2004):

- "Initially assess each student's knowledge/skill level and preferred learning style.
- Provide an array of high-quality, interactive learning materials and activities.
- Individualize study plans."

The same team also recommends computer technology towards achieving the goal of "greater access to a range of appropriate, personalized and individualized learning, teaching, and resources." Authentication concerns can be easily removed with solutions like the one implemented by Pace University, "which provides secure testing for online learners through a proctoring network" (Moore, 2004). Education co-exists with other concepts and entities in human society such as government, economy, security, family life, and others. As such, it is influenced and is influencing the global society. Internet-based education transcends political borders, societies, and cultures. Consequently, it is much more likely to influence and be influenced by global trends. The same is true by all things Internet-based, especially those with direct impact on education or impacted by it such as business, career and communication.

Human nature dictates (sic) that societies prefer to be democratic rather than dictatorial. One of the most visible attributes of democracy is the right to individual expression. While universities are far from displaying dictatorial inclinations they do impose a rigid regiment of student performance evaluation – especially in distance learning courses.

Presently most distance-learning providers are for-profit companies. It is only natural that they seek to minimize overhead and maximize revenue. An essential component of their business philosophy is standardization of teaching and evaluation practices. This need is imposed in part by the distributed nature of their faculty. However, it is fair to expect that sooner or later one online university will adopt the a-la-carte philosophy of teaching and testing. Such a school will instantly acquire a leadership position because it will be able to morph each program and class to suit any set of student circumstances and educational goals.

Technologies like Internet 2, multimedia enabled mobile devices, ubiquitous wireless communication coupled with the maturing of the global economy paradigm will fuel the need for highly specialized individuals. The industrial revolution of the 19th century should serve as a sound reminder that when societies evolve they require their members to change and adapt. An essential component of such adaptation is the ability to specialize in areas, which did not exist earlier.

Since the concept of the free market economy is gaining unstoppable momentum worldwide, it translates into a survival of the fittest approach to individual skills, performances and future prospects. Against this background it is imperative that individuals are afforded the opportunity specialized certification in highly specialized fields. Such a feat would be impossible to accomplish without an individualized approach to individual performance evaluation.

In summary, educational institutions must align themselves with the emerging trend of personalizing and individualizing business services, business requirements, and aspects of personal life. The Internet has evolved from a communication tool to a lifestyle, an essential component of the fabric of global society. It provides a venue for personal expression and direct peer-to-peer communication using text, voice, and video.

Online distance education providers have a unique opportunity to drive the evolution of personalized evaluation rather than driven by it. In the 19th century, the industry demanded it. In the 21st century, the students (and soon industry) will demand it. Brick and mortar universities are watching as the enrollment in online schools soars. Soon online schools will be watching as enrollment in online schools, which offer personalized degrees, and evaluation soars. However, in a democratic, capitalistic society individuals and institutions alike have the right to fall behind and miss opportunities.

References

A Comparative Analysis of Learning Object Content Models.
Available online at
http://www.cs.kuleuven.ac.be/~hmdb/publications/files/pdfve
rsion/41315.pdf

ABET Open University, accessed February, 2005, http://mba-open-
university.net/

Advanced Distributed Learning website. Accessed March 9, 2005 at
http://www.adlnet.org/index.cfm?fuseaction=abtadl

.

Alonso, F., López, G., Manrique, D., & Viñes, J. (2005). An
instructional model for web-based e-learning education with a
blended learning process approach. British Journal of
Educational Technology, 36(2), 217-235. Retrieved Sunday,
May 21, 2006 from the Academic Search Premier database.

American Institutes for Research, 2002. The Digital Disconnect: The
Widening Gap Between Internet-Savvy Students and Their
Schools. Prepared for the Pew Internet & American Life
Project. Retrieved on February 1, 2005 from

http://www.pewinternet.org/pdfs/PIP_Schools_Internet_Repo
rt.pdf

Armstrong, A. (2004). *Instructional design in the real world – a view
from the trenches*

Atkinson R. K., Derry S. J., Renkl A., Wortham D. (2000) Learning
from examples: instructional principles from the worked
examples research. Review of Educational Research. 70:181–
214.

Banu (2001). Development Of Noninvasive And Quantitative
Methodologies For The Assessment Of Chronic Ulcers And
Scars In Humans. Wound Repair & Regeneration, 9(2), 123-
132. Retrieved Sunday, June 11, 2006 from the Academic
Search Premier database.

Bennett, K., & McGee, P. (2005). Transformative power of the
learning object debate. Open Learning, 20(1), 15-30.
Retrieved Sunday, May 21, 2006 from the Academic Search
Premier database.

Bowden, C., & Akdeniz, Y (1999)., "Cryptography and Democracy:
Dilemmas of Freedom," in Liberty eds., Liberating
Cyberspace: Civil Liberties,

Human Rights, and the Internet, London: Pluto Press, 1999, 81-125.

Bradford, M. (2005), *Motivating students through project-based service learning*, Retrieved February 1, 2005 from http://www.thejournal.com/magazine/vault/A5181.cfm

Buchanan, J., & Thompson, S. (1973). A Quantitative Methodology to Examine the Development of Moral Judgment. Child Development, 44(1), 186-189. Retrieved Sunday, June 11, 2006 from the Academic Search Premier database.

Caprioli, M. (2004). Feminist IR Theory and Quantitative Methodology: A Critical Analysis. International Studies Review, 6(2), 253-269. Retrieved Sunday, June 11, 2006 from the Academic Search Premier database.

Carliner, S. (2001, Summer). Administering Distance Courses Taught in Partnership with Other Institutions, Online Journal of Distance Learning Administration, 4(2), retrieved February, 2005, from http://www.westga.edu/~distance/ojdla/summer42/carliner42.html

Carstens, A., Beck, J. (2005). Get Ready for the Gamer Generation.
TechTrends: Linking Research & Practice to Improve
Learning; May/Jun2005, 49 (3), p22-25.

CCLA (2004). *Cyber Snooping*. Retrieved, February 13, 2005 from
http://www.ccla.org/privacy/cybersnoop.html

Chong Ho Yu, C. (2001). Misconceived relationships between logical
positivism and quantitative research, Research Method
Forum, 2003. Available online at
http://www.aom.pace.edu/rmd/2002forum.html

Clark, R. (2003). *Building expertise. Cognitive methods for training
and performance improvement*. Washington, DC: Book of
International Society for Performance Improvement.

Clark, R. C., Mayer, R. E. (2002) Does practice make perfect? In:
Clark R. C., Mayer R. E., editors. E-Learning & the Science
of Instruction. Jossey-Bass Wiley; San Francisco, CA
Colero. L. (2002). A Framework For Universal Principles of Ethics,
retrieved February 2005 from The W. Maurice Young Centre
for Applied Ethics, University of British Columbia website,
http://www.ethics.ubc.ca/papers/invited/colero.html

Conrad, K. (2000). Instructional design for web-based training. Amherst, MA: HRD Press.

Corbit, M. (2005).Moving into Cyberspace: Game Worlds for **Learning,** Knowledge Quest Sep/Oct 2005, 34 (1), p18-22

Creswell, J.W. (2002). Research design: Qualitative, quantitative and mixed methods approaches. Thousand Oaks, CA: Sage Publications.

Cyrs, T. E. (1997). Competence in teaching at a distance. *New Directions for Teaching & Learning,* (71), 15-18

Danchak, M., 2005 "Using adaptive hypermedia to match web presentation to learning styles", in Elements of quality online education: into the mainstream, eds J. Bourne and J.C. Moore. Needham, MA

DeKanter, N. (2005). Gaming Redefines Interactivity for Learning. TechTrends: Linking Research & Practice to Improve Learning, May/Jun 2005, 49 (3), p26-31.

Denis, J. L. & Lomas, J. (2003). Convergent evolution: the academic and policy roots of collaborative research. Journal of Health Service Res Policy (8)2.

Dolog, P., Sintek, M, 2004. Personalization in Distributed e-Learning Environments. Retrieved February 1, 2005 from http://www.www2004.org/proceedings/docs/2p170.pdf

EC Team, (2004, Spring). ALN Principles for Blended Environments, The Sloan-C newsletter.

Federal Trade Commission (2004*). Financial Privacy: The Gramm-Leach Bliley Act.* Retrieved February 13, 2005 from http://www.ftc.gov/privacy/glbact/index.html.

Federal Trade Commission (2000). *Privacy Online: Fair Information Practices In The Electronic Marketplace. A Report to Congress.* Retrieved February 13, 2005 from http://www.ftc.gov/reports/privacy2000/privacy2000.pdf.

Friesen, N. (2003) There objections to learning objects. Available online at:phenom.edu.ualberta.ca/~nfriesen (accessed 30 September 2004).

Gall (2003).

Garrison, D. R., & Archer, W. (2000). A transactional perspective on
    teaching and learning: A framework for adult and higher
    education. Amsterdam: Pergamon

Gearhart, D., (2001). Ethics in Distance Education: Developing
    Ethical Policies. Retrieved February 13, 2005 from
    http://www.westga.edu/~distance/ojdla/spring41/gearhart41.h
    tml.

Graves, W. H. (2004). Academic redesign: accomplishing more with
    less, Journal of Asynchronous Learning Network (8)1.

Griffin, C., & Phoenix, A. (1994). The Relationship between
    Qualitative and Quantitative Research: Lessons from
    Feminist Psychology. Journal of Community & Applied
    Social Psychology, 4(4), 287-298. Retrieved Sunday, June
    11, 2006 from the Academic Search Premier database.

Hadwin, A. F., Winne, P. H., Nesbit, J. C. (2005). Roles for software
    technologies in advancing research and theory in educational
    psychology. British Journal of Educational Psychology,
    75(1), 1-24.

Häggman-Laitila, A., & Pietilä, A. (1998). Life control and health in
    view of qualitative and quantitative research. International

Journal of Nursing Practice, 4(2), 103-112. Retrieved Sunday, June 11, 2006 from the Academic Search Premier database.

Harden, R. (2005). A new vision for distance learning and continuing medical education. Journal of Continuing Education in the Health Professions, 25(1), 43-51. Retrieved Sunday, May 21, 2006 from the Academic Search Premier database.

Harden, R., & Hart, I. (2002). An international virtual medical school (IVIMEDS): the future for medical education?. Medical Teacher, 24(3), 261-267. Retrieved Sunday, May 21, 2006 from the Academic Search Premier database.

Hirumi, A. (2005). In Search of Quality. Quarterly Review of Distance Education, 6(4), 309-329. Retrieved Sunday, May 21, 2006 from the Academic Search Premier database.

Hodgins, H.W. (2002) The future of learning objects, in:D.A.Wiley (Ed.) The Instructional Use of Learning Objects (Agency for Instructional Technology, Association for Educational Communications and Technology). Bloomington, Indiana.

Hollingsworth, S. (1992). Learning to teachf through collaborative conversation: a feminist approach. American Educational Research Journal, 29(2), 373-404.

Hunsaker, L. & Johnston, M. (1992). Teacher under construction: a collaborative case study of teacher change. American Educational Research Journal 29(2), 350-372.

iTeamwork.com web site. Accessed on March 25, 2006 at http://www.iTeamwork.com.

IVIMEDS. (2006). Accessed online on May 27, 2006 at http://www.ivimeds.org/news/demonstrator.html

Jackson, H. F. and Chernish, W. N. (2004). Designing Distance Learning to Reach Underserved Populations. Retrieved February, 2005 from http://www.celt.lsu.edu/CFD/E-Proceedings/ChernishJackson21.htm

Johnson, R. B. (2005). Program research and evaluation. Accessed online on December 17, 2005 at http://www.southalabama.edu/coe/bset/johnson/660lectures/kirk2.htm

Jones, E. T., Lindner, J. R., Murphy, T.H., & Dooley K.E. (2002). Faculty Philosophical Position Towards Distance Education: Competency, Value, and Educational Technology Support. Online Journal of Distance Learning Administration, 5(1), Spring 2002

Kelly, H. (2005). **Games**, Cookies, and the Future of Education. Issues in Science & Technology, Summer 2005, 21 (4), p33-40.

Kirkley, S. E., Kirkley, J. R (2005). Creating Next Generation Blended Learning Environments Using Mixed Reality, Video *Games* and Simulations. TechTrends: Linking Research & Practice to Improve Learning May/Jun 2005, 49 (3), p42-89.

Koerner, M.E. (1992).The cooperative teacher: an ambivalent participant in student teaching. Journal of Teacher Education, 43(1), 46-56.

Lasseter, M & Rogers M (2004). Creating flexible e-learning through the use of learning objects. Educause Quarterly. 27(4). Retrieved May 25 from http://www.educause.edu/apps/eq/eqm04/eqm04410.asp?bhc p=1

Laurillard, D. (2002). Rethinking university teaching: a conversational framework for the effective use of learning technologies. Routledge Falmer, London..

Lave, J. and Wenger, E. (1991). *Situated learning: legitimate peripheral participation.* Cambridge University Press: Cambridge, 1991.

Lehmann, T, and Granger, D.(1991). Assessment at Empire State College-strategies and methods used in evaluating distance education. In Rudolf Schuemer, ed., Evaluation concepts and practice in selected distance education institutions. Hagen, ZIFF, Fern Universitaet. Retrieved February 10, 2005 from. http://www1.worldbank.org/disted/Management/Benefits/qa-03.html

Lim, C. P., Nonis, D., Hedberg, J. (2006). Gaming in a 3D multiuser virtual environment: engaging students in Science lessons. British Journal of Educational Technology, Mar 2006, 37 (2), p211-231.

Lorenzo, G., Moore, J (2002). The Sloan consortium report to the nation: five pillars of quality online education. Retrieved February 10, 2005 from http://www.sloan-c.org/effective/pillarreport1.pdf

Mackintosh, W., Mason, R., & Oblinger, D. (2005, February 1). An ODL perspective on learning objects. Open Learning, pp. 5,13. Retrieved Sunday, May 21, 2006 from the Academic Search Premier database.

Maxwell, J.A. (1992). Understanding abd validity in educational
　　　research. Harvard Educational Review, 62(3), 279-301

MacLaren, I. (2004). New trends in web-based learning: objects,
　　　repositories and learner engagement. European Journal of
　　　Engineering Education, 29(1), 65-71. Retrieved Sunday, May
　　　21, 2006 from the Academic Search Premier database.

Mayer R E. (2001). What good is educational psychology? The case
　　　of cognition and instruction. Journal of Educational
　　　Psychology, 2001, vol. 36:83–88.

Mendels, P. (2000). *Online ethics should begin in classroom,*
　　　educators say. Retrieved February 1, 2005 from
　　　http://faculty.plattsburgh.edu/stewart.denenberg/csc372/articl
　　　es/ethics%20education.html

McCullagh, D. (2004). *US Wants to Tap VoIP*. Retrieved February
　　　13, 2005 from
　　　http://www.globetechnology.com%2Fservlet%2Fstory%2FR
　　　TGAM.20040108.gtvoip0108%2FBNStory%2FTechnology
　　　%2F&ord=1108385394951&brand=globetechnology&force_
　　　login=true

MERLOT (2006). Accessed online on May 15, 2006 at
http://www.merlot.org.

Merrill, D. (1983). Component display theory. In C. M. Reigeluth
(Ed.), Instructional design theories and models: an overview
of their current status. Hillsdale, NJ: Erlbaum, 279–333.

Metros, S. (2005). Visualizing knowledge in new educational
environments: a course on learning objects. Open Learning,
20(1), 93-102. Retrieved Sunday, May 21, 2006 from the
Academic Search Premier database.

MIT OpenCourseware. (2008). Massachusetts Institute of Technology
website, accessed February, 2008,
http://ocw.mit.edu/index.html.

Moore, J. C. (2004). A synthesis of Sloan-C effective practices,
Journal of Asynchronous Learning Networks, Retrieved May
16, 2006 from
http://www.aln.org/publications/jaln/v9n3/v9n3_moore.asp

Nielsen, J. (2000). Useit website. Accessed online on December 17,
2005 at http://www.useit.com/papers/heuristic/

Northcentral University web site, http://www.ncu.edu/learner_area/

NRCC web site. Accessed on December 17, 2005 at
http://de.nr.edu/de/profile.asp

OfficeLive web site. Accessed on March 25, 2006 at
http://officelive.microsoft.com

Palloff, R. M. and Pratt, K. (2001). Lessons from the cyberspace
classroom: the realities of online teaching San Francisco, CA.
: Jossey-Bass Publishers.

Paras, B., Bizzocchi, J. (2005). Game, Motivation, and Effective
Learning: An Integrated Model for Educational Game Design

Parrish, P. (2004). The Trouble with Learning Objects. Educational
Technology Research & Development, 52(1), 49-67.
Retrieved Sunday, May 21, 2006 from the Academic Search
Premier database.

Pegler, C. (2004). Postgraduate Certificate in Teaching and Learning
in Higher Education. Retrieved February, 2005 from the
Open University of the UK website,
http://iet.open.ac.uk/coursesonline/PCLTHE/interactive/down
load/h850cg2004.pdf

Petula, B., 2004. Leveraging Technology for Personalized Assessment/Instruction. Retrieved February 1, 2005 from http://www.nationaledtechplan.org/bb/discuss2.asp?mode=ga &catID=201&status=approved&bm=239-0

Prawat, R.S. (1991). Conversations with self and settings: a framework for thinking about teacher empowerment. American Educational Research Journal, 28(4), 737-757.

Reeves, J and Kimbrough , D. (2004, June).Solving the Laboratory Dilemma in Distance Learning Chemistry, Journal of Asynchronous Learning Networks 8(4), retrieved February, 2005 from http://www.sloan-c.org/publications/jaln/v8n3/v8n3_reeves.asp

Rossman, P. (2002). The future of higher (lifelong) education: a vision for a century ahead, planning for all worldwide, a holistic view. Online book. Retrieved March 1, 2005 from http://ecolecon.missouri.edu/globalresearch/

Salomon, G. (1991). Transcending the qualitative-quantitative debate: the analytic and systemic approaches to educational research. Educational Research, 20(6), 10-18

Savery, J. R., Duffy, T. M. (2001). Problem Based Learning: An instructional model and its constructivist framework. CRLT Technical Report No. 16-01, Indiana University, Bloomington IN.

Schaffer, S., Douglas, I. (2004). Integrating Knowledge, Performance, And Learning Objects. Quarterly Review of Distance Education, 5(1), 11-19. Retrieved Sunday, May 21, 2006 from the Academic Search Premier database.

Schulman, M. (2004). Internet Ethics – I Have A Question. An Exploration On How Students Use The Web For Research. Retrieved February 13, 2005 from http://www.scu.edu/ethics/publications/submitted/schulman/internet-research.html.

Schweber, C. (2005) *A tipping point for online education?* Retrieved March 10, 2005, from http://www.sloan-c.org/publications/view/v4n3/pdf/v4n3.pdf

Simson, S. E. (2005). What Teachers Need to Know about the Video Game Generation. TechTrends: Linking Research & Practice to Improve Learning; Sep/Oct 2005, 49 (5), p17-22.

Spinello, A. A.(2003). *CyberEthics – Morality and Law in Cyberspace.* Jones and Bartlett Publishers, Sudbury, MA.

Spinello, R. A. & Tavani, H. T. (2004). Readings in CyberEthics. Sudbury, MA: Jones
and Bartlett Publishers.

Squire, K.,Giovanetto, L., Devane, B., and Durga, S. (2005). From Users to Designers: Building a Self-Organizing Game-Based **Learning Environment**. TechTrends: Linking Research & Practice to Improve Learning; Sep/Oct 2005, 49 (5), p34-74.

Standen, P. J., Brown, D. J. (2005). Virtual Reality in the Rehabilitation of People with Intellectual Disabilities. CyberPsychology & Behavior; Jun2005, 8 (3), p272-282.

Swan, K. (2001). Virtual interaction: design factors affecting student satisfaction and perceived learning in asynchronous online courses. Distance Education 22(2)
http://ecolecon.missouri.edu/globalresearch/index.html

Sweller J., van Merrienboer J. J., Paas F. G.(1998) Cognitive architecture and instructional design. Educational Psychology Review vol. 10:251–257.

The Java™ Tutorial (2006). Accessed online on May 27, 2006 at
http://java.sun.com/docs/books/tutorial/java/concepts/object.h
tml

The University of Phoenix web site, Retrieved March 6, 2005 from
http://online.phoenix.edu/FAQ.asp#q17.

The University of Texas at Dallas, Executive MBA Program.
Accessed February, 2005 at The Economist website,
http://www.economist.com/globalexecutive/education/executi
ve/profile2.cfm?id=utdglemba

U.S Department of Education, National Center of Educational
Statistics. 2000. Internet access in U.S. public schools and
classrooms: 1994-1999. Retrieved February 1, 2005 from:
http://nces.ed.gov/pubs2000/2000086.pdf

Verbet, K. & Duval, E (2002). Towards a Global Component
Architecture for Learning Objects

Vockell, E. (2004) Development of Thinking Skills, Chapter 7 of
Educational Psychology: A Practical Approach. Online
Resource Accessed on December 4th, 2004 at:

http://education.calumet.purdue.edu/vockell/EdPsyBook/Edp
sy7/edpsy7_development.htm

Wagner, E. D. (1997), Interactivity: From agents to outcomes. *New Directions for Teaching & Learning,* (71), 111-117.

Weller, M. (2004). Models for large scale e-learning, Journal of Asynchronous Learning Networks, Retrieved March 1, 2005 from http://www.sloan-c.org/publications/jaln/v8n4/v8n4_weller_member.asp

Wiley, D. A. (2000).Connecting learning objects to instructional design theory: A definition, a metaphor, and a taxonomy. Retrieved May 12, 2006 from http://www.reusability.org/read/chapters/wiley.doc

Wilhelm, P., & Wilde, R. (2005). Developing a university course for online delivery based on learning objects: from ideals to compromises. Open Learning, 20(1), 65-81. Retrieved Sunday, May 21, 2006 from the Academic Search Premier database.

Writely.com web site. Accessed on March 25, 2006 at http://www.Writely.com.

www.ingramcontent.com/pod-product-compliance
Lightning Source LLC
LaVergne TN
LVHW011225080426
835509LV00005B/319